GOD'S SECRET

Overcoming addiction, suicide, and the world

B O B B Y   S K Y

ISBN 978-1-64458-724-9 (paperback)
ISBN 978-1-64492-289-7 (hardcover)
ISBN 978-1-64458-725-6 (digital)

Christian Faith Publishing, Inc.
832 Park Avenue
Meadville, PA 16335
www.christianfaithpublishing.com

Printed in the United States of America

Here you will find only the truth…

Dedication

I dedicate this book to Jesus my Lord and Savior. Who found me in my wilderness and lead me to unconditional love and spiritual truth. I would like to dedicate this book to anyone struggling with addiction, suicide, and depression. I also would like to dedicate this to my father Robert, my mother Venus, and to my fellow Millennials. May this book reach those who are in spiritual bondage. May their eyes be opened so that they may see behind the veil. Father God, I ask that you lead them in the way of truth and freedom. In Jesus's name, Amen.

A practical guide on fasting and stepping
into the presence of God.

A Love Letter from God

My child,

You may not know me, but I know everything
    about you (Psalm 139:1)
I know when you sit down and when you rise up
    (Psalm 139:2)
I am familiar with all of your ways (Psalm 139:3)
Even the very hairs on your head are numbered
    (Matthew 10:29–31)
For you were made in my image (Genesis 1:27)
In me you live and move and have your very
    being (Acts 17:28)
For you are my offspring (Acts 17:28)
I knew you even before you were conceived
    (Jeremiah 1:4–5)
I chose you when I planned creation (Ephesians
    1:11–12)
You were not a mistake, for all your days are writ-
    ten in my book (Psalm 139:15–16)
I determined the exact time of your birth and
    where you would live (Acts 17:26)
You are fearfully and wonderfully made (Psalm
    139:14)
I knit you together in your mother's womb
    (Psalm 139:13)
And brought you forth on the day you were born
    (Psalm 71:6)

I have been misrepresented by those who don't
know me (John 8:41–44)

I am not distant and angry but am the complete
expression of love (1 John 4:16)

And it is my desire to lavish my love on you (1
John 3:1)

Simply because I am your father and you are my
child (1 John 3:1)

I offer you more than your earthly father ever
could (Matthew 7:11)

For I am the perfect father (Matthew 5:48)

Every good gift that you receive comes from my
hand (James 1:17)

For I am your provider and I meet all of your
needs (Matthew 6:31–33)

My plan for your future has always been filled
with hope (Jeremiah 29:11)

Because I love you with an everlasting love
(Jeremiah 31:3)

My thoughts towards you are as countless as the
sand on the seashore (Psalm 139:17–18)

And I rejoice over you with singing (Zephaniah
3:17)

I will never stop doing good to you (Jeremiah
32:40)

For you are my treasured possession (Exodus
19:5)

I desire to establish you with all my heart and all
my soul (Jeremiah 32:41)

And I want to show you great and marvelous
things (Jeremiah 33:3)

If you seek me with all of your heart, you will
find me (Deuteronomy 4:29)

Delight in me and I will give you the desires of
your heart (Psalm 37:4)

For it is I who gave you those desires (Philippians 2:13)

I am able to do more for you than you could possibly imagine (Ephesians 3:20)

For I am your greatest encourager (2 Thessalonians 2:16–17)

I am also the father who comforts you in all your troubles (2 Corinthians 1:3–4)

When you are broken hearted, I am close to you (Psalm 34:18)

As a shepherd carries a lamb, I have carried you close to my heart (Isaiah 40:11)

One day I will wipe away every tear from your eyes (Revelation 21:3–4)

And I will take away all the pain you have suffered on this earth (Revelation 21:3–4)

I am your father, and I love you even as I love my son, Jesus (John 17:23)

For in Jesus, my love for you is revealed (John 17:26)

He is the exact representation of my being (Hebrews 1:3)

He came to demonstrate that I am for you, not against you (Romans 8:31)

And to tell you that I am not counting your sins (2 Corinthians 5:18–19)

Jesus died so that you and I could be reconciled (2 Corinthians 5:18–19)

His death was the ultimate expression of my love for you (1 John 4:10)

I gave up everything I loved that I might gain your love (Romans 8:31–32)

If you receive the gift of my son Jesus, you receive me (1 John 2:23)

And nothing will ever separate you from my love again (Romans 8:38–39)

Come home and I'll throw the biggest party heaven has ever seen (Luke 15:7)

I have always been father, and will always be father (Ephesians 3:14–15)

My question is... will you be my child? (John 1:12–13)

I am waiting for you (Luke 15:11–32)

Love your dad,
Almighty God

Contents

Chapter 1

The terrorist & the cave

"Nearly all men can stand adversity, but if you
want to test a man's character, give him power."

Tony Stark AKA Ironman finds himself in a predicament (I can
relate). He's trapped inside a cave with a band of terrorists. The leader
of these madmen demands that Tony use his gift (making weapons of
death) to build a missile called the "Jericho". The terrorist has an evil
agenda and Stark knows it.

Make the missile or die. Tony knows that he is dead either way.
Whether he makes the missile or not, one thing is for sure. Stark is a
dead man! He has nowhere to turn to, no place to hide, and is now
forced to face the truth. What truth? The truth is that it was Tony's
fault that he was in the cave in the first place. During his capture,
Tony spots a missile in the enemy's camp and it reads "Stark tech-
nologies". One of the weapons that he had created in his Malibu
mansion was now in unworthy and malevolent hands. Was this the
terrorist's fault? Absolutely not! Tony knew it too. For the first time
in his life, he had to face his mistakes. His first mistake was wasting
his precious time. He was a womanizer and spent countless hours in
revelry.

Even though he worked long hours on his craft, there was still
time he wasted chasing after the wind and pleasures of this world.
The time that he wasted was the "bazooka" of his problems. Those

choices always ended up hurting the people closest to him including himself. If that wasn't bad enough, his second and greatest mistake was the "atomic bomb" that could potentially destroy nations of people. His greatest mistake was that he sold his gift (weapons of death) to the highest bidder. He didn't protect his gift but instead he whored it out to the people who had the deepest pockets. This was clearly displayed in a scene right before his kidnapping. Tony showed up to a missile demonstration with his custom-made Armani suit, up chuck reflux, and with a scotch in his hand. He was careless and ready to sell a weapon of death to Benjamin Franklin and his cloned twin brothers. Tony resembled someone on Wall street without any thought or care of consequences. He had completely sold his soul and his gift for his own selfish interests. Had he been more selective about who his buyers were, the terrorists would never have had one of Stark's missiles in their possession.

Tony was forced to face this reality. Instead of passing the buck, Tony accepted responsibility for his business, his gift, his choices, and his bleeding heart. His bleeding heart was now dying and it was full of greed and lust. Tony desperately needed a metamorphosis. He needed a change, a transformation. A desire to evolve and the passion to get up off the ground and to stop eating the dirt. No more compromising and settling for good enough or second best. No one is exempt from the consequences of choices that we make. Tony was in his greatest trial that he had ever faced. It wasn't a financial crisis. It wasn't a real estate deal gone sour. It wasn't the tragic death of his parents.

It wasn't drugs or alcohol. It wasn't a failed relationship or marriage. It wasn't criticism from haters or gossip. His technology business wasn't failing. He wasn't struggling with homelessness. His life's biggest trial in the cave was simple. His trial was facing the truth. Stark died in that cave but it was not a physical death. He let go of his selfish ambitions and made a choice that changed his life forever. He knew if he continued living the same lifestyle, multitudes of others would be destroyed including himself. Innocent people would die without any hope, help, and no way of escape.

Tony repented of his sins and thus the Ironman suit was birthed. You see, he always had that Ironman suit idea deep inside him but it could never manifest because he was too busy serving himself. There was no need for the Ironman suit because Tony was only interested in revelry and chasing good times while ignoring the needs of others. Once he realized there was a need in the world for peace and protection for the helpless, his inner genius ignited. It was official, Stark died a spiritual death in that cave. His doctor friend asked him "is this the end of the great Tony Stark?" He proved to his friend that it was not the end. Tony had become reborn in his inner man and the Ironman suit was an outer manifestation of an inward commitment. He made a commitment to serve other people no matter what it cost him. After that cave experience, he spent his free time perfecting and protecting his suit. He became loyal to one woman and sacrificed his life to save others. He wasn't perfect, but he raised the standard in his life as well as the people that he associated with. He became a brand creation and life was never the same. He faced the truth about who he really was and found something on the inside of him. He said to himself: "I can't be this way anymore. I can't live like this. I need to change."

> "Therefore, if any man be in Christ, he is a new creation: old things are passed away; behold, all things have become new."
> —2 Corinthians 5:17

Every single person has an Ironman suit idea on the inside of them that is screaming to come out and make itself known in this dark world.

Unfortunately, that gift (everybody has a gift) will lay dormant until you decide to live for others and not for yourself like Tony did. You do make a difference! Every choice that you make matters! The question is will you continue to live for yourself or will you lay your life down for Jesus and for the betterment of others? Will you let your Ironman suit die with you or will you give birth to something greater? The choice is yours and it always has been. Deciding to follow Jesus is a choice that you will have to make for yourself. No one can force you. God doesn't force himself on anybody, that's called rape, not relationship. I just hope that you come to know how much he loves you and he will change your life if you'll let him. You are special and very important. No one past, present, or future will ever have your finger print.

You are uniquely and wonderfully made. God went through great lengths to make you unlike anybody else. I dedicate this book to you and share with you my personal journey when God found me. I never believed in religion and most churches out there are dead. What I'm talking about here is having a real relationship with God and finding out who you really are, why you are here on this planet, and the great things that you are capable of. Your dream is too important! I'm tired of seeing the devil lie to people and tell them they aren't worth anything. People are dying both physically and spiritually. God is crying over it!

I care about you too much to not tell you the truth. I have to tell you what God saved me from and what he did for me. If I don't say anything to anyone, I would be selfish. It's not about book sales, the big houses, or nice cars. You've heard all kinds of things that people and the enemy have said about you. Throw that behind you now. While I was going through it, I wondered why I went through all the hell that I did. I realize now why it happened. I went through all of it for you. I went through all of it so that one day I could write to you and tell you the good things that God has done for me. The truth is that he doesn't love me more than he loves you. What he did for me, he'll do for you too, if you'll let him. The Lion of Judah waits for you. He knocks at your door. Will you let him in? Is it really so hard to believe in God? To believe in Jesus? To believe in love? He knocks at your door. You can turn him away. You can invite him in. He's always been there waiting, by your side… What will you do?

Chapter 2

Hermione isn't clever!

"Truthful lips endure forever, but a lying tongue
is but for a moment."
                                                —Proverbs 12:9

Has anyone ever talked negatively about you behind your back? Was
there ever a time somebody said something about you that you knew
was false? Maybe a friend or family member spread an untruthful
message about you. Perhaps a stranger or even an enemy made a
verbal attack against you so that you would suffer in some way. Can
you think about a time that this has happened to you personally?
A verbal assault leaves a mark, especially if it isn't a true statement.
This reminds me of an old saying "sticks and stones may break my
bones but words will never hurt me". This couldn't be further from
the truth. Words do hurt people. They have the power to inflict
injury or to remedy it. My friends, if this has happened to you personally, you share the same struggle God has been putting up with
in today's world and in the modern American culture. He has been
presented to us in a certain way that makes him appear malevolent
and malicious. To non-believers, it's common for them to view God
as a harsh creator. With movies, shows on Netflix, Facebook, music,
and a variety of other channels, people have this distorted view of
who God really is. In this chapter, we are going to examine a couple
of scenarios in which God has been presented falsely to you. Before

we dive in, it must be noted here, that everything in life is designed to give us a false reality and distract us from the truth. What truth? The truth that God loves you and wants to have a relationship with you! That however, is not the message we receive. What is the message that we hear? God is evil. God destroys. God is angry with us. God is egotistical and on some sort of power trip. Etc. Where can we see this? Let's use an example that is fairly recent. Hmm. How about the movie "Noah" starring Russell Crowe, Emma Watson, and Jennifer Connolly? The movie hit the big screen in March of 2014. In the movie, a girl named Ila (Emma Watson AKA Hermione Granger) gives birth to twin girls. Noah seizes the twins and after much inner conflict (he believes God told him to murder the two innocent babies), spares them upon looking at his granddaughters and only feeling love. Now, this is the story of Noah (according to the movie). If you've ever seen the flick, it is easy to see how a person could question God. It really puts God in this evil light, almost like he has no heart at all.

Here's a question to consider. If God wanted to wipe out all of humanity, why would he save Noah and his family by having him build an ark? Why
not just let them all perish together in the flood? Well folks, that's because the real story of Noah did not happen like the movie "Noah" portrayed. In the bible, in the book of Genesis it says:

[15] Then God said to Noah, [16] "Come out of the ark, you and your wife and your sons and their wives. [17] Bring out every kind of living creature that is with you—the birds, the animals, and all the creatures that move along the ground—so they can multiply on the earth and be fruitful and increase in number on it."

[18] So Noah came out, together with his sons and his wife and his sons' wives. [19] All the animals and all the creatures that move along the ground and all the birds—everything that moves on land—came out of the ark, one kind after another.

[20] Then Noah built an altar to the Lord and, taking some of all the clean animals and clean birds, he sacrificed burnt offerings on it. [21] The Lord smelled the pleasing aroma and said in his heart: "Never again will I curse the ground because of humans, even though[a]

every inclination of the human heart is evil from childhood. And never again will I destroy all living creatures, as I have done.

²² "As long as the earth endures, seedtime and harvest, cold and heat, summer and winter, day and night will never cease."

So, do you see it now? In the real story, God intended for Noah and his family to "be fruitful and increase in number". Don't believe everything you see in movies.

Sorry Hermione but you aren't clever!

Dear Reader,

> I'm going to challenge you with a thought. Have you ever judged somebody before you really met them? A stranger? A coworker? A neighbor perhaps? I have! I'm guilty! I confess that I've even judged God before I met him and knew who he really was. At one point in my early twenties, I believed that God didn't care, was egotistical, and on some sort of power trip.
> Oh, how wrong I was!

King Solomon Is Evil Or Is He?

On the surface, it's really easy to look at a story in the bible and call it evil. Just take your pick of the popular examples. How about the story of Abraham? He was going to sacrifice his son Isaac because God asked him to? Ok?!? Yeah, Abe is a lunatic and God is out of control with sadistic issues. Well, that is how I used to think. I would look at a story like that in the bible without really dissecting it. I would just call God "evil" and be done with it. Because we all know that murder is evil right? Or how about the story of Solomon? I want to highlight this story in particular because it involves an innocent baby. I'm sure we can all agree that killing an innocent infant is wrong right? If you disagree, I strongly recommend that you don't read this book any further. Here's a story of how God used Solomon to do a wonderful thing for a desperate mother.

The Lord Makes Solomon Wise

⁵ One night while Solomon was in Gibeon, the Lord God appeared to him in a dream and said, "Solomon, ask for anything you want, and I will give it to you."

⁶ Solomon answered:

My father David, your servant, was honest and did what you commanded. You were always loyal to him, and you gave him a son who is now king. ⁷ Lord God, I'm your servant, and you've made me king in my father's place. But I'm very young and know so little about being a leader. ⁸ And now I must rule your chosen people, even though there are too many of them to count.

⁹ Please make me wise and teach me the difference between right and wrong. Then I will know how to rule your people. If you don't, there is no way I could rule this great nation of yours.

¹⁰⁻¹¹ God said:

Solomon, I'm pleased that you asked for this. You could have asked to live a long time or to be rich. Or you could have asked for your enemies to be destroyed. Instead, you asked for wisdom to make right decisions. 12 So I'll make you wiser than anyone who has ever lived or ever will live.

¹³ I'll also give you what you didn't ask for. You'll be rich and respected as long as you live, and you'll be greater than any other king. ¹⁴ If you obey me and follow my commands, as your father David did, I'll let you live a long time.

¹⁵ Solomon woke up and realized that God had spoken to him in the dream. He went back to Jerusalem and stood in front of the sacred chest, where he offered sacrifices to please the Lord[c] and sacrifices to ask his blessing.[d] Then Solomon gave a feast for his officials.

Solomon Makes a Difficult Decision

[16] One day two women[e] came to King Solomon, [17] and one of them said:

Your Majesty, this woman and I live in the same house. Not long ago my baby was born at home, [18] and three days later her baby was born. Nobody else was there with us.

[19] One night while we were all asleep, she rolled over on her baby, and he died. [20] Then while I was still asleep, she got up and took my son out of my bed. She put him in her bed, then she put her dead baby next to me.

[21] In the morning when I got up to feed my son, I saw that he was dead. But when I looked at him in the light, I knew he wasn't my son.

[22] "No!" the other woman shouted. "He was your son. My baby is alive!"

"The dead baby is yours," the first woman yelled. "Mine is alive!"

They argued back and forth in front of Solomon, [23] until finally he said, "Both of you say this live baby is yours. [24] Someone bring me a sword."

A sword was brought, and Solomon ordered, [25] "Cut the baby in half! That way each of you can have part of him."

[26] "Please don't kill my son," the baby's mother screamed. "Your Majesty, I love him very much, but give him to her. Just don't kill him."

The other woman shouted, "Go ahead and cut him in half. Then neither of us will have the baby."

[27] Solomon said, "Don't kill the baby." Then he pointed to the first woman, "She is his real mother. Give the baby to her."

[28] Everyone in Israel was amazed when they heard how Solomon had made his decision. They realized that God had given him wisdom to judge fairly.

If you only read the part of the story about Solomon asking for a sword so that he may cut the child in half, you miss the rest of the lesson here. God had granted Solomon supernatural wisdom and was able to use it for the good of others. They don't say this in the bible, but Solomon had no intention of harming the baby. His real intention was to get the child back into the arms of the biological mother and that was the end result. No harm was done and the truth came to light. So, what's the point here? It's simple. God is into saving people and babies. How do I know that? Because he saved me…

Chapter 3

I got 99 problems but a stitch ain't one

"I can see how it might be possible for a man to look down upon the earth and be an atheist, but I cannot conceive how a man could look up into the heavens and say there is no God."

—Abraham Lincoln

"Are you ready to pray?" my mother would ask. "Yes mommy" would always be my immediate response. Prayer would occur every night just before bedtime when I was a young, skinny, adventurous, and curious 6-year-old boy. My days consisted of playing outside with my friends from early morning until sunset. It is an understatement that my mother had a very hard time getting me inside for anything. I can recall skipping meals to be outside and she would quite literally have to threaten me to come inside to eat. I loved being outside! Climbing trees, riding bikes, street hockey, hide & seek, playing in streams in the woods, basketball, and anything else we could think of was the norm growing up. Coming up with new games, testing my 6-year-old body's physical limits, and worrying my mom half to death with my adventures was a normality for me. Our nightly ritual involved a single and simple prayer before bedtime. Sometimes I wondered if we only prayed because she was so worried about me during the day. We never went to church or read the bible but she made it a point to recite the Lord's Prayer with me before I would drift off to a sweet sleep:

<u>Our father, who art in heaven,</u>
<u>Hallowed be thy name.</u>
<u>Thy kingdom come,</u>
<u>Thy will be done,</u>
<u>On earth as it is in heaven.</u>
<u>Give us this day our daily bread.</u>
<u>And forgive us our trespasses,</u>
<u>As we forgive those that trespass against us.</u>
<u>And lead us not into temptation,</u>
<u>But deliver us from evil.</u>
<u>For thine is the kingdom,</u>
<u>And the power, and the glory,</u>
<u>Forever and for forever</u>
<u>Amen.</u>

We prayed like that every night when I was 6 years old and continued with it faithfully every evening until I was 8. That's it! That was my entire prayer life growing up! When I moved in with my father at the age of 8, we would have conversations of God (some of them quite intelligent and deep) but there was absolutely zero prayer after that. To give you an idea of how worldly I was, let me tell you a story. When I was 8 years old, my father took a job at a local pool hall during the weekdays. He was retired at the time he took this job, but in his day, he was a phenomenal pool player. Every day after school, he would show me how to play. He would teach me how to hold the cue, where to put my elbow, use angles, and how to use English on the cue ball. We had a fun time arguing because he tried repeatedly to get me to shoot right-handed. I am right-handed in most things, but when it came to playing pool, shooting left-handed came more natural for me. Looking back, I'm sure it was a funny sight looking at an eight-year-old shooting pool left-handed who could barely see over the table. This was my life for over a year. After school, I would shoot pool for several hours until it was time to go home. Every day,

I was progressing in my skills and the time came that I entered my first tournament. I was 9 years old and I entered a weekly "adult" pool tournament that was held every Friday night. I recall there were about 35–40 people who entered and I was really excited to be able to compete. I came in 3rd in that tournament! My 9-year-old self was devastated and I cried aggressively because I didn't win. "Keep practicing son" my father told me. So, for another month I practiced harder than I ever had. I entered my 2nd tournament after practicing a little over a month. There were more people in this tournament but I won! I'll never forget the man who was in his 30s or 40s that I played in the final round. After I hit the 9 ball in the pocket to win the tournament, he stormed out of the pool hall, started yelling, and pushed the front door open with obvious frustration. Imagine that! A 9-year-old boy winning an adult pool tournament. I took my $200 winnings, bought a celebratory Laffy taffy (I'm nine, don't judge me) and spent the rest on Nintendo 64 video games. For 6–7 years I would wash, rinse, and repeat this process many times. While some of my peers from school were in a church pew on Sunday mornings, I dwelled in the mist of juke box music (ACDC, Aerosmith, Nickel back, kid rock, George strait Etc.), the aroma of lit up Marlboro reds, and inappropriate cursing. This led me to alcohol, drugs, and rebelling against authority. It's no surprise either, because both of my parents were addicted to opiates and other drugs at that time. My father was hurt because he never met his dad. To make matters worse, my father's mom left him at an orphanage at an early age, and even signed him over to the army at the age of 17 to go to war in Vietnam. To make it worse, when the American troops came back from the war, they were spit on and rejected. That left him with feelings of being abandoned, unloved, and with an orphan spirit. He was hurt to say the least. He tried to fill the void in his heart with drugs, women, gambling, business, pornography, and entertainment but only to find it empty. Dad even sold potent prescription pills for extra money (he tried to hide it from me but I knew). Mother also had it tough growing up. She was the victim of persistent sexual abuse from her stepfather as well as physical abuse during her whole childhood. While I was growing up, Mom was either doing speed, taking pills, or drinking. She would read every self-help book that she could find and even listened to Oprah's "worldly wisdom" to try to find peace. Like my father, mom tried to fill the emptiness in her heart with the things of this world. I followed my parents' pattern of drug use because it was all I knew. It wouldn't be until I turned 24 years old that I would start praying by myself for the first time. That is 16 years without a prayer life. Looking back on those prayer times with my mother (even back then she was using drugs), I'd like to think those prayers kept me safe even as I grew into a teenager and eventually as an adult. I was a young and wild 8-year-old with no fear of the world, but no 8-year-old boy should have the option to roam around freely like I did. Without parental supervision, that freedom definitely set me on a course of exploration in regards to the world and what it had to offer me. In 2008, I was really growing through a rough time in every area of my life. I was 17 years old at the time and was struggling with promiscuity, drugs, alcohol, pornography, rebelling against my father, and all matters of my schoolwork were a huge after thought. I was in a constant state of revelry and it showed. I hit a breaking point, something shifted in me, and I just wanted to end my life. Depression was so strong on me and at that time I could not tell you where it was coming from. It was like I was fighting against some unseen force that I was oblivious to (funny enough that is not far from the truth). One spring evening in April of 2008, I had decided that I would take my life into my hands and end the struggle. I got into one of my dad's less expensive cars that he had. It was a white 1980s Buick park avenue. That night I said to myself "It will be ok; he's gone at the casino and won't be back for hours". I smelled like cheap Arkansas grown marijuana as I chugged my last beer of the six pack that my friend Cody had bought me just hours earlier. I also had a few Percocet in my system as well. The fact that I could stand, walk around, and make any type of decision was a miracle in itself. I walked out the front door with the keys of my father's white 1988 Buick Park Avenue with one thought in mind "It will be over soon". I drove around the city of Fort Smith Arkansas completely inebriated. As I drove, I pondered on where would be the best place for my demise. Time was skipping in the incoherent condition that

I was in, and I found myself near downtown Fort Smith close to the Creek more park. "This is it"! I gunned the gas pedal to the floor. My heart raced faster as my father's car climbed in speed. The old Buick had reached a speed of 60 mph. and then:

BOOM!!!!!!!!!!!

"Are you ok!!!!???" (Man's voice)

Where was I? Am I dead? What is going on? I opened my eyes and closed them in a split of a second. In that split second, I knew I was in the car and I heard the sound of the man's voice again:

"The ambulance is on its way, hang on!!" (male stranger)

Then darkness...

What's going on? (Me)

You've been in a serious car accident, you're very lucky to be alive, someone loves you. Try to relax, we are stitching you up right now. (Male doctor)

Then darkness again...

"He's only eighteen years old. Has his family been notified?" (Male doctor)

"Yes, his father is on his way right now" (Female doctor)

"This is really a nasty gash on his forehead, it will take at least 50 stitches to sew it back up." (Male doctor)

In the pit of my stomach, I felt shame and guilt. My dad is on his way to the hospital right now? What will he do? How could I have been so selfish? What is wrong with me? Why did I do this? And why in God's name am I still alive? These thoughts began swimming around in my immature 17-year-old brain...

Faded into darkness once again...

My eyes opened slowly as if I was coming out of a yearlong coma. I had never been in a coma before but I imagine this is what it felt like. I laid there on the hospital bed with heavy eyelids, entire body drained of energy, and the electrical signal that was relayed to my brain through my eye's retina when the light struck it was very uncomfortable. I closed my eyes and opened them repeatedly to get used to the light again. My eyes scanned across the room to make out any visible figure and I noticed an object hovering next to me...

"There you are! You are lucky to be alive son, do you know how drunk you were young man??" (Male doctor)

"No" was all I could muster up the courage to say (Me)

The doctor's words that followed after would stay with me for the next 10 years of my life…

"King size drunk! Your blood alcohol level was .55! Accident aside, the alcohol alone should have killed you! Blood alcohol content becomes life threatening at .40 and you were at .55!

> "I will never leave you or forsake you"
> (Hebrews 13:5).

"Were you trying to kill yourself?" (Male doctor)

The other female doctors and nurses all stood beside him in complete bewilderment. Maybe this doctor was acting in a way they had never seen before. Maybe they were flabbergasted that a 140 pound 17-year-old kid had survived such a high intake of alcohol and such a rough accident. Everything about the situation was chaotic at best but the next word that I spoke came out with embarrassment and without any hesitation…

"Yes" (me)

"Well, we will deal with that later but you need to rest. We've stitched up your forehead and it should heal nicely. There are 55 stitches in it right now and we will set up an appointment to take them out. We took a photo of your head before we stitched you up, do you want to see it?" (Male doctor)

Feeling completely vulnerable and exposed, I let out a weak… "Ok" (me)

He reached for his phone, pulled up the picture, and handed me his phone. Even though I was heavily medicated with morphine, staring at my head that was split wide open gave me the chills.

"We can send it to you so that you can keep it or we can delete it. What do you want to do?" (Male doctor)

Looking back on that statement, I realize the doctor was trying to teach me some humility about the poor choices I had made.

"Delete it" I replied. "I never want to see that again". (Me)

I handed him back his phone with my hand which was shaking involuntarily…

"Ok. There it is gone. Also, you should know, you have pretty severe nerve damage to your right leg. We will prescribe some medication for you take home with you but I should warn you that it won't help you very much. The physical therapy we scheduled for you will help, but you will have to fight through the pain that you're going to have. It won't be easy." (Male Doctor)

"I understand" (me) I uttered those words with the help of the morphine haze I was in.

Looking back, God used doctors to heal my leg. I didn't have the faith back then to believe in healing in my body without medicine. As I laid in bed, they brought me a brochure of a mental facility in little rock Arkansas. They had planned on sending me there for a mental evaluation. After some debate and convincing, the hospital staff decided not to send me to a mental institution for my suicide attempt. I told them "I will never do anything like that again". They must have believed me because I was discharged from Mercy hospital in Fort Smith AR and sent home to bed rest with periodic physical therapy and AA meetings. The next two months were the most arduous, hopeless, and pain filled in my life. My pillow would become my best friend filled with many tears of agony. I did not know anything about nerve damage but I learned quickly! I did not think it was possible for a human being to hurt that much. Take a sword, set it ablaze with unquenchable fire, and run it up and down on the inside of my leg. That's what it was like! Screaming into my pillow became a routine for the next 2 months as I cried out to God to get better. It was so bad that if I laughed, coughed, or sneezed that it would spark the pain to begin. Talk about a complete slap in the face! I can't laugh!!? Are you kidding me!?? My friends would come to visit me and we could watch comedies but I'd have to fight the humor. My father would usually be in the next room hearing his son in agony. I was completely imperceptive to anything other than the pain I was experiencing. I'm positive that my dad had a really rough time just being around me. He was quite a figure to look at. 6 feet tall, 18-inch arms and a long ponytail. He had an affinity for nice jewelry like gold chains, watches, and rings. He looked like someone who just walked off the set of the Sopranos. Even though he had a tough exterior, I can't imagine what it was like for him to hear his only son scream in pain like that. Years later I would ask him about it and he just said "son, I just didn't know what to do or how to help you. I was not prepared for something like that". I recall there were times he left the house for awhile just to escape all of the screaming. I don't blame him. Physical therapy was tough, and AA meetings were pointless. Being in Alcoholics Anonymous in Arkansas is a humorous thing. All we did is listen to people tell their drunken stories. Each one was wilder than the next and a strategy on how to deal with Alcoholism was non-existent. "It was a joke" I thought to myself. I never shared any of my stories and I let the others brag about their experiences. I remember lying in bed after a meeting one day and was pondering about my life. I wondered how I had allowed myself into such a painful predicament. I was fighting something, but I did not have the slightest idea as to what it was. Today, I know exactly what it was that pushed me to make a life-threatening choice. While I was in that bed, I decided that I was going to change and be different. I needed a fresh start with new people and new places. "Everything new" I thought to myself. After my body healed as much as it could, I moved out of my dad's place and went to live in Olathe Kansas which was just on the outskirts of Kansas City. For the next couple of years, I did everything as best as I could. I received my GED at a local community college (JCCC) in overland park Kansas. I was hired at my first big boy job at a check company called Deluxe Corp where I would be promoted twice. In retrospect, I made a decent living as a 20-year-old. I had a new girlfriend, a new beautiful black and white blue-eyed Siberian husky, a new car, and a new place of my own. It was a peaceful time in my life where nothing went wrong. The most strenuous thing I had to deal with was my dog "jewels" and her A.D.D issues. Life on the outside was better, but I was still taking opiates and drinking. I still had a hole in my heart that I couldn't fill. I eventually broke up with my girlfriend of 2 years because of my selfish addictions. A couple of months later she began dating again. She, her boyfriend, and his small children were killed July 4th 2013.

Alcohol was the root cause of the car accident. Then my father had passed away from heart failure in February of 2014. I had been reacquainted with Drinking, drugs, and smoking all over again. I moved back to Fort Smith and landed a job at the nearby casino (which is where my father passed away. I took a job as a bartender during the evenings. The only fresh air I would really get is the trips to the local fenced in Dog Park. One day when I was at Walmart in a Vicodin induced haze, I was strolling through the electronic section browsing at the new movies looking for one that I may purchase. The new wolverine? "Seen it". The wolf of Wall Street? "I have it". And then out of the corner of my eye something caught my attention. "The Son of God" Why am I looking at this? I never went to church and most definitely never read a bible. And God most definitely despises me, right? "Buy it, what does it matter?" I thought to myself. After watching the movie, I started to get curious and purchased the whole bible collection on DVD. Spiritually, I was starting to open up a little. I admit I watched that collection while being high on opiates. God was drawing me to himself.

> No one can come to Me unless the Father
> who sent Me draws him;
>
> —John 6:44

For the first time in my life, when no one was around, I prayed to God:

"God, I'm hurting because of my dad and because he's gone. Could you please do something for me today to show me that he is ok, that he is at peace, that you are real, that angels are real, and that we all have angels looking out for us?"

I prayed that prayer during a spring morning in 2015. That particular day, I decided to take a walk. I walked to the library to look at books, walked to the post office, and took a stroll past the golf course in Fianna Hills. My last stop was at a PIC N Tote gas station just a few blocks from my dad's house. Now here's where things started to get interesting. I'm brand new to prayer and didn't really expect anything to happen. Let me point out that I go by "Bobby" but my legal name is Robert. I'm bantering with the cashiers as usual and I'm wearing a ring that my father gave to me as a graduation present. I had the ring customized and had it fitted onto a necklace. The cashier lady immediately noticed it and said "Nice ring! Someone important gave that to you, didn't they?"

"Yes ma'am" I replied. "That's strange" I thought to myself. How did she know that? It wasn't a miracle but sort of funny how she said that with such certainty. I shrugged it off and told myself that she just had a lucky guess. People do it all the time right? Now, the cashiers and I continued on talking for a couple more minutes and then I headed towards the door to leave with my items. The employees at the gas station knew me as "Bobby" and have always called me by that name. As I was leaving, they waved and said in perfect unison "have a good day Robert!" Why did they call me that? At the same time no less? Very bizarre! "People are acting strange today," I remember saying to myself. As I'm walking back to my father's house, I thought about the name "Robert". Yes, it was my legal name. My father went by "Bob" but his legal name was also "Robert". So, I'm walking back to the house thinking about the name "Robert". I walk the few blocks back to my dad's house (which is the last house on a dead-end street). You literally have to go all the way down the road on purpose to get there. I walk up to the porch and go to open the door with my house key when I heard it:

"Look down." (Jesus)

"What's this?" I spoke. There was a coloring book picture laying on the front porch mat so I picked it up and turned the page over. What I saw completely froze me up. I was speechless! It was a picture of a boy all colored in (from a toddler most likely) and it had a title at the top of the page that read: "Robert had a good day."

What?!? How?! You've got to be kidding me!! This is nuts!?!? There is no way!!! How is this possible? Then it dawned on me and I remembered… My morning prayer! I asked for God to give me confirmation that my dad is ok, that God is real, and that we have guardian angels helping, guiding, and protecting us…

"He heals the brokenhearted and binds up their wounds" (Psalm 147:3).

For the first time in a long while, I had some peace about my dad, that God was real, and that my prayers were being answered. Even though I could not see them, there were forces at work beyond my mere human perception. Not long after that, for reasons unknown to me at the time, I prayed for Jesus to take my father's demons out of me. Back then, I couldn't tell you what made me pray. Today, I know it was the Holy Spirit guiding me. The Holy Spirit is not an "it" but a "he". He's a person who speaks. Not a person like us, he's a spirit. Oddly enough, I was scrolling through the television channels later that day and came across something that disturbed me. I should note here that I've never believed in "the devil" up until that point in my life and I had always thought it was a made-up fabrication. I ended up stopping on a show called "true life" that was aired by MTV. This particular episode was about people who were addicted to drugs. What caught my attention was this particular twenty something year old woman. She was addicted to meth or heroin (I can't remember exactly which). In a possessed like state, she was high and mumbling incoherently while the camera crew was filming. I shake my head that people actually film this stuff just to make a buck. But what she said just startled me. Completely isolated in the country and in front of a broken-down trailer, she uttered the following words "All hail satan!!!" Here is this lady and she was murmuring all sorts of things that I'm sure no one could make out. The only thing she said that was audible was "all hail satan". It floored me. MTV even had those 3 words in caption but everything else she uttered was inaudible. I felt this conviction that what I was witnessing was very real! A couple of days later, when I was curled up in bed, I drifted off to sleep. When I woke up, I went to the mirror next to my bed to fix my hair before going out. As I'm standing there, I glanced in the mirror and what I saw was completely and utterly jarring. My reflection was of my body but with a demon face attached to it! This demon face was staring at me with a growl like expression. It looked like it wanted to devour and eat me. It resembled a Jeepers Creepers/Sméagol/ gremlin/lord

Voldemort mutant combo face. This creepy face was looking back at me in the mirror. I was a little freaked out to say the least but I could not look away. This thing was demonic and gruesome! And it was so strange to see my body in the mirror with a demon head staring back at me! For some reason, I had no fear and peace overcame me. All I remember saying in my head was "Jesus Christ". This actually lasted for what seemed like 5–10 seconds. I just kept on repeating the name in my head. Just the name "Jesus". While I was standing in front of the mirror, all of a sudden, everything went blank. I went from standing directly in front of that mirror and then something mysterious happened. I was now back in my bed! What? I'm back in bed?!! How is that possible?

"You may ask me for anything in my name, and I will do it." (John 14:14)

Chapter 4

The blind side

"The greatest trick the devil ever pulled was
convincing the world that he doesn't exist"

Shortly after that, I decided to go to the exact spot where I had my
accident just 6 years ago. My high school buddy and his girlfriend
told me that I had hit a tree that night. Must have been a pretty
strong tree for me to hit it at 60 MPH. I thank God it was a tree and
not another human being. As I drove to the accident site, I ques-
tioned why I felt so compelled to do so. What was I expecting to see
or find? I mean, it's been six years. Any remnants of a 17-year old's
stupidity should be wiped away by now. The things we do follow us
and whisper in our ears "I'm reminding you what you did". Those
words stop when we learn from it, grow, and turn away from our selfish ways. I stood in wonder looking at this impressive Sycamore tree
that I had a tango of destiny with 6 years ago. The tree was on church
ground! The accident site was located at a Christian church in Fort
Smith Arkansas. Was I spared my life because I was on holy ground?
Maybe or maybe not. Was I spared because God would not allow it?
If so, why? All these thoughts consumed me for the day with no possible way of figuring it out so I dropped it. I'm just happy to be alive
and that no one else was hurt. At this point in my life, the depression
of my father's death subsided exponentially. I felt better but I was still
living worldly. Even though I was opening up spiritually, I started

dabbling in worldly ways of doing it. I tried practicing the law of attraction (the secret by Rhonda Byrne), binaural beats, meditation, positive affirmations, chakra work, yoga, and studied Buddhism. Once, I even had my neighbor come over to perform a ritual with incense, sage, and crystals. It's crazy to see that my prayers had been answered by the creator of heaven and earth but I was still searching for God in all of the wrong places. Grief, depression, and drugs have a way of keeping us blind even when we see the truth and the proof of his manifestation power. God answered a very personal prayer of mine in a time of mourning. I knew then that he was real because of the picture that showed up on my doorstep. Truth is a person and his name is Jesus Christ of Nazareth. When you know Jesus personally, you know the truth of this world. He shows you himself. With my neighbor, my intention was to just open up spiritually and find out more. He had told me about spirit guides that minister to you and help you with your life's purpose. What my friend did is what New Agers call "channeling". He was able to channel another spirit into his body and I was left there sitting on my living room floor talking to God knows what. When this spirit entered my neighbor's body, he looked me right in the eye and began speaking to me: "So, I heard you are seeking for truth and guidance" (unknown spirit)

"Yes." (Me)

I was perplexed at the interaction that was taking place. This spirit told me his name but I have long forgotten it. It was evident that anyone with two working eyeballs would know that my friend was now gone and that I was communicating with something else entirely. My friend's body was there but he was possessed. His face and countenance changed. I was not afraid but I had no clue who or what I was talking to and the next part of the conversation disturbed me greatly…

I understand that this all sounds unimaginable. Also, I want to indicate here that I was not under the influence of any hallucinogenic drugs of any kind. Lastly, I didn't receive any brain damage in my car accident when I was 17 (at least none that I'm aware of). Ha-ha! In all seriousness, my heart's desire is to just tell you the truth and leave you with the choice of believing it or not. I'm not here to convince you but to share with you my story and all of the good things God did for me (you'll read about them later). Let me continue with the rest of this story (it's strange, I agree).

"Well good thing you are talking to me because I know all kinds of truth. You are really lucky to be able to talk to me. You should know that I'm not going to waste my time with you if you don't listen to me. "Carol" does everything I say, so if you want my help you must listen".

(Unknown spirit)

I was puzzled because this spirit called my neighbor "Carol" but his name was "Carlos" I replied "Ok, well what truth do you have to offer?" (Me)

"For starters, did you hear about that church that burned down 2 weeks ago?" (Unknown Spirit)

"No, I haven't, why?" (Me)

"That was me! I did it! He said Grinning devilishly (Unknown Spirit)

"What? Why would you do something like that?" I replied perplexed and bothered (Me)

"Because I can and it was fun!" (Unknown spirit)

After I heard that, I became really silent. I researched this particular church later on and realized that this spirit was telling the truth. The church had been burned down by a fire and no one knew the cause. This was absolutely sinister and I could not believe I was having a conversation with what was obviously a demon. This entity actually admitted to wreaking havoc on churches. I was done with this conversation and we just ended up in this weird staring contest. After what seemed like 1 minute of a staring match, the mischievous and malevolent spirit broke the silence…

"Is there anything YOU want to ask or know" (Unknown spirit)

"No, I'm done with you" (Me)

"I'll see you again soon, I'll find you" (unknown spirit)

And then he left and my friend returned

"What happened?" (My friend)

"You're leaving" (Me)

It replayed in my head a few times as I recall the devilish smirk this demon displayed using my friend's body "I'll see you again soon, I'll find you". I whispered to myself as my neighbor walked out my front door "No you won't".

Later I realized why that spirit kept calling my neighbor "Carol" instead of his real name "Carlos". In my own life, I've always had very strong feelings to do drugs, sleep around with women, watch pornography, drink, party, and chase money. The key word here was "felt" or "feelings". However, my feelings lied to me. I realized that my addiction was more than just a feeling that I grew up with. Drugs, to me, were like a powerful magnet. It was a strong pull that would hit me consistently and then I'd be off to the races chasing my next high. My sin problem was drugs which is also known as sorcery or the Greek word which is pharmakeia. For my neighbor, his sin was homosexuality. The demon that was talking to me through Carlos, his name was homosexuality. Demons have names. The demon I contended with at that point in my life was called addiction. That spirit would make me "feel" like getting high. It was an intense feeling that I had zero control over. Carlos's demon gave him feelings to live a homosexual lifestyle. Both scenarios and feelings are lies. There's a reason why these so-called feelings can feel so strong in our lives and that we feel absolutely powerless to overcome them. The word of God warns us:

> For we do not wrestle against flesh and blood, but against principalities, against powers, against the rulers of the darkness of this age, against spiritual hosts of wickedness in the heavenly places.
>
> —Ephesians 6:12

> **'Do not turn to mediums or seek out spiritists, for you will be defiled by them. I am the LORD your God. (Leviticus 19:31)**

Chapter 5

Favor isn't fair

"Service to others is the rent you pay for
your room here on earth."
　　　　　　　　　　　　—Muhammed Ali

God was working on me, but I still had a long way to go. After I
left my bartending job at the casino, I took an office job that only
paid me 8 dollars an hour. It was pure poverty and impossible to pay
the bills. One day in December of 2014, Jesus moved on my heart
to give away a tenth of my income for the first time. In the bible it
says we should tithe 10% of our income. I was down to my last 25
dollars. I wasn't planted in a church yet and had no clue what tithing really was. My lights were about to be shut off, my birthday had
just passed, and Christmas was just around the corner. With faith, I
donated my last 25 dollars to FEED THE CHILDREN. It broke my
heart knowing that these children were starving and it felt good to
help someone in dire straits. As soon as I donated the money, inter-
nally I felt a shift in my spirit. Something was unlocked or released. I
can't explain it but I just felt different immediately. I still had no way
of paying my light bill and any hope of buying some food for myself
was now gone. "Ah well at least I'll eat something at our Christmas
party". My employer was holding a Christmas party at the nearby
convention center where we could eat and they were going to give
away prizes throughout the night. I was working at my job through

a temporary agency. My team lead and district manager informed us that only "full time employees are eligible for prizes and it does not apply for temporary associates". They were giving away TVs, money, electronics, free trips, restaurant vouchers, and many other items. I was eating my full plate of food and talking with a neighbor when the district manager took out a microphone and said: "Okay now it's time to draw names for the secret balloon giveaway."

With a room of about 200 tables, we all turned our attention to her as she called out the names. She started calling them out one by one and then the next one stunned me...

"BOBBY"!!!

I walked up confused but no one said anything or mentioned the obvious fact that I was a temp and should not have won. She lined up about 10 people including myself in a straight line. On her mark, we were to grab a balloon on the floor, pop it, and grab a ticket that was placed inside each balloon. The ticket would have writing on it telling us what we won.

"ONE, TWO, and THREE..."

We all ran toward our balloon and I popped mine with slight hesitation.

POP!!!

I knelt down and picked up the white ticket inside of my balloon and it read:

"$250.00"

Wow! You've got to be kidding! God is good! He multiplied my seed ten times over!

> "Bring the whole tithe into the storehouse, that there may be food in my house. Test me in this," says the LORD Almighty, "and see if I will not throw open the floodgates of heaven and pour out so much blessing that there will not be room enough to store it."
>
> —(Malachi 3:10)

Today, I always tithe ten percent of my gross income to my church that I attend. Before I pay any bill, my tithe gets paid first. Off the top! Back then, Jesus asked me to give my ten percent to the feed the children organization and I obeyed him. He honored my giving even though it wasn't the "storehouse" which is the church. He knew that I would honor him faithfully with my finances in the years to come. It's like Jesus was saying to Father on my behalf "I know he didn't tithe his money in the church this time, but he will eventually. He will understand the principles of sowing seed into good soil and reaping a harvest in a couple of years. Let's honor this seed and multiply it because he hearkened unto my voice. Let's give him a tenfold return now and we can teach him the full principle of tithing later." And the father honored Jesus's request on my behalf! I thank him that I can sow my seed into good soil now and not some other church where all they want is your money. There's nothing wrong with helping organizations like feed the children, but I didn't know what tithing really was back then. Giving is a wonderful privilege and it honors God when we do it.

Chapter 6

The Epidemic

"Our lives begin to end the day we become
silent about things that matter"

Suicide is a Leading Cause of Death in the United States

→ According to the Centers for Disease Control and Prevention (CDC) WISQARS Leading C auses of Death Reports, in 2018:

- o Suicide was the tenth leading cause of death overall in the United States, claiming the lives of over 48,000 people.
- o Suicide was the second leading cause of death among individuals between the ages of 10 and 34, and the fourth leading cause of death among individuals between the ages of 35 and 54.
- o There were more than two and a half times as many suicides (48,344) in the United States as there were homicides (18,830).

This was an article that came out by the Guardian weekly on sept 3rd 2017:

The number of drug overdose deaths in the US increased by 21% last year, according to new statistics—with synthetic-opioid fatalities more than doubling in number. The National Center for Health Statistics, a division of the Centers for Disease Control and Prevention, (CDC) estimates that drug overdoses killed 64,070 people in the US last year, a rise of 21% over the 52,898 drug overdose deaths recorded in 2015. The epidemic of drug overdoses is killing people at almost double the rate of both firearm and motor vehicle-related death. The statistics posted on the CDC w ebsite are the latest available on the gathering opioid crisis. The agency says they will be updated on a monthly basis. Much of the increase in fatalities is blamed on the synthetic opioid fentanyl, which is typically used for pain management during surgery or in end-of-life settings and has a marked depressive effect on the respiratory system. Along with other synthetic opioids, it is blamed for 20,145 deaths last year, significantly above the 15,446 attributed to heroin or the 14,427 attributed to opioid pills alone. The figure for synthetic opioids in 2015 was 9,945. According to analysis published in the CDC's 31 August edition of Morbidity and Mortality Weekly, "approximately half of the increase in deaths involving heroin after 2013 is attributable to increases in deaths involving use of both heroin and fentanyl". The CDC journal concluded that the opioid overdose epidemic resulted in the deaths of approximately 300,000 people in the US during 1999–2015, including

33,000 in 2015. "The first wave of deaths began in 1999 and included deaths involving prescription opioids. It was followed by a second wave, beginning in 2010, and characterized by deaths involving heroin. A third wave started in 2013, with deaths involving synthetic opioids, particularly illicitly manufactured fentanyl (IMF). IMF is now being used in combination with heroin, counterfeit pills, and cocaine." Unlike heroin, illicit fentanyl and its ingredients are largely manufactured in labs overseas, particularly in China. It can be up to 100 times more potent than morphine, and the fentanyl molecule can be tinkered with to create even more powerful drugs and subvert regulation. It has been revealed in documentaries that "practicing" doctors admit to lying and prescribing fentanyl to non-cancer patients in order to generate kick back bonuses for themselves from the pharmaceutical companies.

My dear mother passed away in January 2017 due to an overdose of taking fentanyl. In my grief, my aunt Marie (my mother's sister) suggested that I come to stay with her and my cousins for a while to be with family. I accepted with a numb "ok". I was now in Dallas Texas. I landed a job at Metro PCS. It was a great call center full of friendly and genuine people. I made it through training and worked for a couple of weeks but my spirit was shattered. I couldn't explain it then, but I knew something was missing. Worst of all, the job entailed that we fix all of our customer's problems who called in with "empathy". Empathy!? Really!?? How in God's name can I have genuine empathy for someone whose data is throttling because they refuse to read a book once in a while? I'm sorry buddy, but I don't feel empathy for you because you're upset that you've used 22 GBS of internet data in one week. How could I? I felt chained, trapped, enslaved, and like I was in some sort of invisible cage. "I can't do this" I said softly to the department manager. "I'm sorry, I used to be really good at a job like this, but I'm not capable of giving genuine empathy right now". My manager was more than understanding and she thanked me for my honesty. She would share with me the details of her own childhood, her experience with abuse, and all that her and her family had overcome. I started to realize that we all have struggles that we need help to overcome.

Chapter 7

Beam me up Scotty

"If you're going through hell, keep going."
—Winston Churchill

"God, give me shelter." (Me)

I heard him say... "Keep walking in the same direction that you are going. Keep the same path, you're nearly there' (God)

Little did I know what miracles god had in store for me at that time, I was just hungry, fatigued, and discouraged in every sense. All I replied with was a dumbfounding and puzzled:

"Ok" I said (me)

Nearly there? What does that mean? I had no clue what to think but just continued on walking.

And wouldn't you know it, there was a homeless shelter. A homeless shelter? Samaritan Inn shelter is located in McKinney Texas and it was on my path of directions that I had written down on paper! I find it odd to this day that this shelter would help me as much as it did. Generational curses would leave me here and I will be forever grateful for it. It was on my path, like it was meant to be. Crazy!

"You will stay here" (God)

"Hmm. Well, it's not like I am going to live here. I just need a place to sleep." (Me)

Or so I thought...

"We don't have any beds available right now but you can come back tomorrow at 11:00 AM" (The volunteer lady behind counter)

"God, I thought you said that I was going to stay here but they don't have any beds available" (Me)

"Wait" (God)

Tired and frustrated, I walked across the street to a nearby base field that looked abandoned. Night over took the day and I was left in the darkness with a chilly breeze and the night's sky for company. I looked into the clear sky with my hands on the baseball fence and thought of my losses, pain, and hopelessness. What I whispered next would change my life forever: "Jesus, I surrender to you, take my life, it's yours" (Me)

That night I curled up on the bench in the dugout and tried to get some sleep. I rested 30 minutes total which is a generous estimate. Ah well, I just need to make it to the morning and then hopefully they'll have a bed open in the morning…

"Sorry sir, we don't have a bed open, you'll have to come back tomorrow" (volunteer woman)

Back to the field again.

I couldn't possibly sleep on that bench again. I needed to find somewhere else to try to find some shut eye. Plus, it was getting pretty chilly at night and I didn't have a blanket or jacket to keep warm. I had ditched my bag of clothes at a donation box before I arrived. I literally had nothing. I scouted the nearby area for a warmer place to sleep. The bathroom maybe? "How did I get here?" I thought to myself. My brief prayer to Jesus came to my mind but fleeted quickly. Nothing about my situation made any sense to me. But I was tired. I found a spot in the corner, laid my backpack on the ground, and shut my eyes…

I'm in a Multi-level garage. I'm completely alone and there are a variety of cars with different colors and models. The ground was shaking furiously and I had a sense that trouble was coming. This was a multi-story car garage at least 50 levels high. Then all of a sudden, cars started falling through the ceiling! They were falling all throughout the garage and dropping one by one closer to where I was standing. BOOM!! The sound of glass shattering and metal hitting concrete echoed through this mystic and monolithic garage with me right in the middle of the chaos. "How do I get out of here?" I thought to myself. Then all of a sudden, someone or something came and touched me. I was lifted up to one of the higher levels in the garage. This was truly sporadic and mind blowing because I was certainly going to die. I was standing at the end of this hallway where there was a tall glass window 20 feet tall that overlooked the city and the surrounding skyscrapers. Directly in front of me was this large ball but it was not physical. The color is hard to describe. I want to say it was a mixture of a dark gray, burgundy, and maroon. The thing was, I felt peaceful around it whatever this was. It was just hovering right in front of the window as if it was waiting for me to do something. I didn't even hesitate. What happened next was truly remarkable. I stepped toward this spiritual ball and outstretched my arms towards it or him or her and we became connected. It was as if I didn't need to hold on with my arms, I just needed to be close enough to it for us to be tied together. Immediately when we linked up together, we shot out of the window and went straight up! This was nothing like I had ever experienced. I was taken up into the second heaven. We're flying through space and the stars in the sky! we're passing at a phenomenal rate of speed.

"Praise God!!!!" (Me)

I kept saying "Praise God" over and over while this was happening. I was in such a peaceful state as I was flying through the heavens! There was no worry or concern and I just rode whatever this thing was that shot me up into space. I've never once said "praise god" in my whole life. And here I was saying it over and over with no care in the world. The colors of the stars and planets were vibrant and clearer than any human can describe. It makes our Ultra 4k televisions look dim in comparison to what I experienced that night. This was not a dream, it really happened…

And then I woke up…

WOOOOAH!!!!! My God! I felt different. Like my destiny has been changed. It was so good and euphoric that I didn't even care that I had just slept inside a public baseball field bathroom. I woke up changed for sure! I made a choice to stay at the Samaritan Inn shelter as soon as they accepted me. I went back every morning every day at 11 AM for well over a week before a bed finally opened up…

God was right when he said "you will stay here". I stayed at the Samaritan Inn for 5 months and learned a great deal about humility.

"For I was hungry and you gave me something to eat, I was thirsty and you gave me something to drink, I was a stranger and you invited me in." (Matthew 25:35)

Chapter 8

Daniel's plan

"I am not afraid of storms for I am learning
how to sail my ship."
—Louisa May Alcott

The people who stayed at the Inn would share their intimate stories with me and my heart was truly broken for them. Many of them didn't have the option to be anywhere else other than a shelter. I chose to leave a "normal" life behind because something on the inside of me told me "there's more". Life had really taken a toll on the residents at Samaritan Inn. Single mothers, fathers with child support debt, war veterans with PTSD, widows, failed actors/models, and just about any personal situation you can imagine dwelt there. I felt really ashamed in thinking that I was the only one with problems. During those months, I grew closer to God, began praying, and reading the bible more. Things were getting better, the shelter's people humbled me, but I still felt stuck. There was something hindering me. I was praying at night in a prayer circle consistently and reading my bible. I was also getting up at the crack of dawn to go pray at the ball field. What's going on God? Funny enough, God was already giving me the answer. I had never done a fast before, but the Lord led me to do a Daniel fast for 12 days. Fruits, vegetables, and water only. I used a natural supplement that was designed to cleanse out the colon as well.

One day, I was researching what a Daniel fast was and then I realized I needed to cut out sugar. It was a big thing for me. I liked my coffee in the mornings. I came across an article on the benefits of green tea and decided to do it but I couldn't just drink it plain. I also stumbled on the benefits of raw and unfiltered honey. "That's it" I thought. Instead of my coffee in the mornings which was loaded with cream and sugar, I'd substitute it for green tea and raw honey. After I made up my mind to do green tea and honey in the mornings, a thought occurred to me: "God it would be nice to have plenty of raw and unfiltered honey for my green tea". I didn't consider that a prayer at the time because I didn't say it out loud but just had the thought in my head…

> "You know when I sit and when I rise; you
> perceive my thoughts from afar."
> —Psalm 139:2

Later that day, a donation came to the homeless shelter (people donated items all the time). I was stunned at what I saw. Someone had donated countless boxes of raw and unfiltered honey. There were so many boxes that I couldn't count them all. There was so much honey that it lasted the entire shelter for months, and I only needed it for 10 days! No one knew my thought but God did. He was just showing off at this point! Ha-ha! The honey was called "nature Nate's" and it had a scripture on the bottle:

> "Thy word is sweeter than honey"
> -Psalm 119:103

Eating fruits and vegetables for 10 days and drinking only water have such amazing health benefits. You may have clear skin, lose weight, and have higher energy levels. I did this fast, lost 18 pounds in 12 days, and I felt very energized.

Isn't it amazing that people willingly and frequently expose themselves to toxins all day every day? This carries a heavy cost and there is a price for living in an artificial society (a synthetic world).

Our bodies are being extremely overworked by constantly having to cleanse these toxins out only to have us keep putting them back in. Now, it doesn't really matter what diet you have. Even if you're someone that eats all 100% organically grown food, most soils around the world are contaminated to some degree and it's very difficult to get food that isn't loaded with heavy metals. If you truly want to live a healthier existence, you are going to have to get those toxins out. This is one step that you can take so that you can enjoy the life God has for you. According to science, the majority of our serotonin (happy hormone) is produced and utilized in our colons. However, on average, most people are walking around with 20 pounds of feces in their stomachs. Serotonin can't thrive in that type of environment because there's too much blockage. "Is this guy suggesting that I go get a colonoscopy"? Before you tuck tail and run, let me assure you that is not what I am suggesting! If any of you have ever experienced one of those, I give you my condolences. You can do a colon cleanse within a 10–2 day eating plan. I personally recommend a Daniel fast where you eat only fruits, vegetables, and drink purified water. With that being said, get advice and approval from your doctor before you take on any type of fast. Foods that I ate personally were lettuce, carrots, tomatoes, apples, oranges, raw almonds, bananas, and blueberries. I ate as much as I wanted but it was only certain foods with nutrients. To be clear, there are several ways a person can fast. In the bible. you have people like Jesus, Moses, and Elijah who fasted for 40 days. I chose a Daniel fast because I couldn't cut out food entirely just yet. If you are looking to really supercharge your spiritual walk with God. I would recommend a Daniel fast along with cleansing your colon. Make sure you stay close to a bathroom as you do this for 10–2 days! Ha-ha seriously!

On the 7th day of my fast, I had a tremendous breakthrough. God showed me what was holding me back and hindering me from having real peace. After being in God for a few years, I've learned that we shouldn't share everything that he shows us with other people. I'll never forget what he showed me during that fast, but it was nothing short of supernatural and it was very personal for me. What I can tell you is that I experienced genuine peace. After it was over, I knew there was supernatural power in fasting and prayer. Prayer! I almost forgot to mention that. You must pray every day while you are on the fast, otherwise it's just a diet. The idea behind fasting is helps you disconnect from the world and connect with God. Abstaining from food helps you hear from him more clearly. It is very hard to do for your first round so be patient with yourself. I'm not here to entertain you but to inform you. There are reasons why we go through things that are tough and there seems to be no answer or solution. Allow God to show you and ask him for his help. There are certain areas in our lives that we won't get victory in unless we fast and pray. That's all you have to do! If you feel like you just keep hitting brick walls in life, go on a fast. Ask God to help you. It really is that easy…

"I ate no pleasant food, no meat or wine came into my mouth, nor did I anoint myself at all, till three whole weeks were fulfilled."
—Daniel 10:3

Chapter 9

The Greyhound Subway

"Greater love has no one than this, that someone lay down his life for his friends."
—Jesus Christ

I'm exhausted, hungry, and spiritually drained as I wait for my bus at the greyhound bus station in Dallas Texas. A series of convoluted events led me to sleeping in the DFW airport for three days straight. I was now waiting another full day for my bus to come and transport me from Dallas to Louisville Kentucky. "Why am I going through this"? "I know you wanted me to move to Louisville God. I heard your voice but why do I have to sit and wait for such a long time to get there? Why have all of my resources dried up and I'm just sitting here waiting?" I was cranky to say the least! As I was praying, I had my head in my lap while I sat on an uncomfortable metal bench. Then I felt a tap on my shoulder:

"Hey are you ok, are you hungry?" (Male stranger)

I raised my head up to look at a man in his 40s to 50s who was genuinely smiling at me.

"Yes, I'm ok" (Me)

"Let's get you some food, how about some subway?" (Male stranger)

There was a subway sandwich shop that was connected to the greyhound bus station and I had a craving for it before this man had showed up.

"That sounds great, thank you sir" (me)

We got up and went to the shop which was 20–5 yards away. When we got to the line, he noticed a man in a wheelchair who was counting his change to pay for his meal.

"Do you have enough?" (The male stranger said)

What happened next completely took me off guard. I immediately perked up to see if what I was witnessing was real. The stranger who I just met lifted up his pant leg and some black object attached to his ankle. "Ankle bracelet" I thought at first. Like the ones a criminal would wear. I looked closer and noticed it wasn't an ankle bracelet at all. It looked like a small black fanny pack. He unzipped this object and pulled out what must have been 100 gift cards and credit cards. "What the!?" I said to myself. He searched through the variety of cards that he had until he found the right one "there it is!" he said. The stranger handed the subway cashier a subway gift card and paid for the rest of the man's meal and for my own. He also paid for several other people and handed them books from the backpack that he was carrying around. I peeked at one and could see that it was a bible. One of those revised versions for easy reading. I figured our time was done as he was feeding people with the plethora of cards that had. In bewilderment, I thanked him for his kindness and he said:

"Let's grab a seat and talk a minute, do you have the time"? (Male stranger)

"Sure" (me)

We sat down at a nearby high-top table for 2.

"My name is Bobby" (Male stranger)

I smiled…

"Me too, my name is bobby" (me)

We laughed briefly about our names and continued on with the conversation. He asked me if I knew Jesus and told him that I did.

"God told me to talk to you Bobby. I was looking around the bus station and I wanted to talk to this lady outside but God kept telling me NO. He said I want you talk to him" (Bobby)

Bobby then pointed at me with his finger and I imagine that he probably thought I was asleep when he first approached me. I was actually praying with my head down for a sandwich.

"I was praying, I wasn't asleep. Why do you think God told you to talk to me?" (Me)

"Because he loves you and you have a calling on your life. You are supposed to minister to people" He paused for a slight second as if he was hearing something "are you going to Louisville Kentucky"?

Completely stunned, I let out a murmuring noise: "Yeah?!" (Me)

"We will get to that in a minute, but for now let me tell you a little about how I got here today. I used to be homeless. I lived in pure frustration, hopelessness, and anger. I cursed God for all of my problems while I was doing drugs, drinking, and just worrying about myself. One day, I had enough and was in a rage and screaming at God with all of my hate…" (Bobby)

As he was telling me this story, I noticed his right eye (my left) was milky. In order not to be rude, I kept my attention on his right eye which was a very blue color. He continued speaking…

"…As I was ranting, a picture fell out of my pocket. It landed in a puddle just behind the garbage can that I was standing next to. I picked up the picture and it was a photograph of a younger version of me! I hadn't had a physical picture in my possession in years. I started crying and sobbing Bobby! I immediately realized that it wasn't God's fault that I was living in hell, it was me!!! I begged God to forgive me and asked him if he could use me. Could you use me father?!? Can you make my life matter? Can you make me somebody?

I sat there just listening and hurting for this man. Tears started building up in his eyes…

"I prayed for him to use me and to make a difference." (Bobby)

I looked at his milky eye again and was pondering what must have happened to it…

"…this eye went completely blind after that night and God did it. He blinded it so that he could use me for other people" (Bobby)

He must have read my mind…

"I go around traveling all over the US and God uses me to feed his people and to bring them to Jesus."

I did not doubt this. His actions clearly displayed his devotion to God and I felt ashamed for my lack of commitment. Hearing about Bobby's testimony and his milky eye was staggering. He would tell me that the homeless people he spoke to had a better reaction to him because of his eye. For some reason they would trust him more.

"I don't know what to say" (Me)

'Every person matters Bobby; we have to learn to stop saying the word "I". God is knocking on your door. He's patting you on the back and saying "Son, I need you". How amazing is that? The creator of the heavens, earth, and all of life wants your help. If you surrender, you will meet people, see places, and experience glory like you never could have imagined. If you do his will, you can then ask him for anything and he will do it! (Bobby)

I sat there speechless and tried my best to absorb everything that Bobby was telling me. He continued on to tell me that he was being persecuted. I wasn't surprised because the devil hates it when we help others.

"There is something you need to know, are you aware of the RFID chip?" (Bobby)

It may sound like an Orwellian nightmare, but the technology to implant RFID chips into human beings and track their every move has been there for years.

[16] And he causes all, both small and great, rich and poor, free and bond, to receive a mark in their right hand, or in their foreheads:

[17] And that no man might buy or sell, save he that had the mark, or the name of the beast, or the number of his name. Revelation 13:16–7

"Yes, it's the mark of the beast! It's a chip that will allow people to buy or sell goods. It is planted on the inside of the human body like the hand or wrist" (Me)

"That's right, and it's already been implanted in people. Certain companies and employees are getting the chip here in the US..." (Bobby)

I broke the flow of the conversation and interrupted Bobby before he could speak anymore

"If anyone gets that chip, it's over..." (Me)

"Yes" (Bobby)

We both looked at each other with pain in our hearts because we knew what it meant. Getting that chip means that person doesn't believe in God and that they choose bondage. We had finished our sandwiches and I watched as he left to go outside to help another one of God's children.

"Wow" I whispered under my breath. I turned around and began to open the book he had given me to read when I heard him yell: "Bobby! I know you are going to Louisville; God is telling me to give you this street name and corner" (Bobby)

He gave the name of two streets of downtown Louisville that I wrote down. He also gave me Galatians 6:9 which says:

"Let us not become weary in doing good, for at the proper time we will reap a harvest if we do not give up."

We hugged and he smiled at me. I watched him walk out the front door of Greyhound bus station ministering to people near a pulled over bus. I looked at my piece of paper with my notes for a split second, looked up, and he was gone...

"Do not forget to show h ospitality to strangers, f or by so doing some p eople have shown hospitality to angels without knowing it."
(Hebrews 13:2)

Chapter 10

Celebrity Worship Syndrome

"Why do you think they call it television?
They want to tell-a-vision"
USA Weekend Magazine

Tragically, most parents are ignorant when it comes to realizing the transformative power that popular media wields over their children, and often remain so, until it is too late. USA Weekend Magazine conducted a massive "Teens & Celebrities Survey" comprising more than 17,000 students in grades 6 to 12 that revealed some alarming trends that document how vulnerable many teens are believed to be when it comes to the influence of Hollywood celebrities. USA Weekend stated that "this generation of teenagers is not satisfied with merely staring at posters or even rubbing shoulders with their favorite stars—they want to be them." This massive survey also found "that teens want to look and act like famous people, and although that has been true through the ages, they're taking more drastic steps to do so. About 60% think teens want to pierce a body part or get a tattoo because a celebrity has." The survey also found that 48% drink alcohol; 47% smoke cigarettes; 25% have babies; 58% get tattoos; and about 40% take drugs all because their teen idols do! Celebrities wield such a considerable influence over the masses that psychologists have given a name to what can become a potentially pathological condition called "Celebrity Worship Syndrome (CWS)." Research has found: "One in three people is so obsessed with someone in the public eye that he or she is a sufferer, say psychologists. And one in four is so taken with their idol that the obsession affects their daily life." Furthermore, studies have revealed: "hardcore CWS sufferers are solitary, impulsive, anti-social and troublesome, with insensitive traits. They feel they have a special bond with their celebrity, believe their celebrity knows them and are prepared to lie or even die for their hero." Psychology Today acknowledged that celebrity worship has taken the place of the worship of God for many people and that teenagers are most susceptible to the condition. Truth be told, we are not dealing with a psychological condition as much as we are dealing with a massive spiritually lost condition known as idolatry. This condition is fostered and propagated by media elites in Hollywood and the music industry alike—and both are effectively changing the face of the world. Tragically, millions of young people have been duped by the idea that they can become gods and wield supernatural powers wherein they can bend and manipulate reality to fulfill their own narcissistic will through an endless salvo of Hollywood productions glorifying the occult. The Lie of White Magic. Our Creator, in His great love and wisdom, has provided us with several severe warnings against dabbling in occult practices and trafficking in the spirit realm. In His desire to protect us from satanic forces, God has repeatedly revealed to us through Holy Scripture that there would be an occult revival in preparation for the Antichrist Kingdom just before the Second Advent of Christ in Glory. (Matthew 24:24–25; 1 Timothy 4:1–4; 2 Tim. 3:1, 6–8; 2 Thess. 2:9–12; Rev. 9:19–21)

But sadly, Hollywood's promotion of witchcraft, and its successful disconnect to satanic powers, has seduced countless youth into Satan's dark web. John Andrew Murray wisely warned: "By disassociating magic and supernatural evil, it becomes possible to portray occult practices as "good" and "healthy," contrary to the scriptural declaration that such practices are "detestable to the Lord." This, in turn, opens the door for kids to become fascinated with the supernatural while tragically failing to seek or recognize the one true source of supernatural good—namely God." (John Andrew Murray, "Harry Dilemma," Teachers in Focus; available from www.family.org)

Prior to the present Wiccan revival, Wicca had gained popularity in the counter culture hippie movement among the youth of the 1960's. Satanist, Nikolas Schreck, who was a leader in the Church of Satan (and who is married to Zeena LaVey, daughter of the now deceased, Anton LaVey, founder of the church of Satan), acknowledged that in the 1960's, witches did indeed acknowledge that they were Satanists:

The Satanic Screen "To the contemporary reader, whose idea of a witch may be influenced by the sweetness-and-light Wiccans who have appropriated the word, the dark aesthetic of the '60s witch must be emphasized. Seeing themselves as sisters of Satan, the majority of that era's witches were a far cry from the current Wiccan movement. Just as today's Wiccans are constantly pointing out indignantly that they are not Satanists, the witchcraft movement of the sixties reveled in its romantically diabolical associations." Nicholas Scheck, the Satanic Screen: An Illustrated Guide to the Devil in Cinema.) Gerald Gardner

Many Wiccans are unaware of the fact that much of their teachings, ceremonial magic and "scriptures" are based on the teachings of Satanist, Allister Crowley. Many of Crowley's ceremonies and teachings were simply reformulated by Gerald Gardner, who is credited as the founder of Wicca and was a member of Crowley's satanic organization, known as the OTO.

Wiccan Creed

Even the Wiccan Reed (aka "counsel" or "advice"), "An' Ye Harm None, Do What Ye Will" was influenced by Crowley's maxim, "Do What Thou Wilt Shall be the Whole of the Law." While many Wiccans seek to disassociate from Satanists for understandable reasons, they have been deceived into believing that there is a difference between good and bad demons and so-called "white" and "black" magic. The sobering reality is that all such magic is from the same Satanic source, whether it is called white, black, red, yellow, green or purple.

An ABC of Witchcraft by Doreen Valente. Even Doreen Valente, the Wiccan high priestess who has had more influence on Wicca than any other woman, admitted that, "The distinction between black and white magic has no validity." (Doreen Valente, An ABC of Witchcraft (New York: St. Martin's Press, 1973, p. 271)

Starling, another Wiccan leader, admitted: "This might actually offend some, but it hides one of the great truths of witchcraft, that there is not white or black magic, there is only magic…" This admission is actually in line with the Word of God, which states that all such magic is rooted in Satan's power (1 John 5:19; Revelation 12:9).

"White" magic is simply a ploy Satan uses to draw in his unsuspecting prey as he leads them to believe they can use occult powers for altruistic purposes. God's Word reveals that Satan doesn't typically appear in all of his naked deformity, but he appears more often than not as an angel of light:

> "And no wonder, for even Satan disguises himself as an angel of light. So, it is no surprise if his servants, also, disguise themselves as servants of righteousness. Their end will correspond to their deeds."
> —2 Corinthians 11:14–15

The Satanic Bible by Anton LaVey who founded the Church of Satan in 1966, admitted in his "Satanic Bible" that there is no real difference between "white" and "black" magic, stating, "White magic is supposedly utilized only for good or unselfish purposes, and black magic, we are told, is used only for selfish or evil reasons. Satanism draws no such dividing line." Lave also stated, "There is no difference between 'white' and 'black' magic, except in the smug hypocrisy, guilt-ridden righteousness and self-deceit of the "white" magician himself." (Anton Lave, The Satanic Bible, New York: Avon Books, 1971, p. 110)

The Satanic Witch by Anton Lavin his book "The Satanic Witch," Lave stated that all witches must, at least, symbolically make a pact with the Devil, "The witch has made a pact with the Devil and through rituals dedicated to him gains her power. In order to be a successful witch, one does have to make a pact with the Devil…" (Anton LaVey, "The Satanic Witch"). LaVey though, as a Satanist, admitted that the media was furthering Satan's designs because witches were continuing to be cast in popular culture as "good" and "benevolent." LaVey actually relished in the idea that the masses were being attracted to Satanism through the popular guise of the "good" witch, "I don't see any true reason to readily discount the movie and TV image of the witch, because I think that whatever popular image is most flattering should be utilized and sustained whenever possible. People will believe what they want to believe and the current image of a witch is the most intriguing and glamorous that has yet to appear."

The Devil's in the Details. It is vitally important that we are not "unaware" of Satan's "devices" (2 Cor. 2:11) lest we be deceived. We are warned by God Himself, "Have nothing to do with the fruit-less deeds of darkness, but rather expose them." (Ephesians 5:11) It is critical that we remember that we are not wrestling against mere human forces, but we are wrestling against the dark, cosmic, satanic forces that are in rebellion to the one true God:

> "For we do not wrestle against flesh and blood, but against the rulers, against the author-ities, against the cosmic powers over this present darkness, against the spiritual forces of evil in the heavenly places."
> —Ephesians 6:12

The scriptures also reveal that Satan is the "ruler of the king-dom of the air" and he is presently guiding the "course of this world" as he is "the spirit who is now at work in those who are disobedi-ent." (Ephesians 2:1–2) Satan and his realm advance occult practices and doctrines by channeling their teachings through human agents. These diabolical teachings appeal to the lost masses as they lead them away from "the truth" by "tickling their ears" and telling them "what they want to hear." (2 Timothy 4:2–4) God clearly revealed in His prophetic Word that in the last days, there would be a resurgence of demonic doctrines taught by "seducing spirits" that will cause some to fall away from the faith:

> "But the Holy Spirit distinctly and expressly declares that in latter times some will turn away from the faith, giving attention to deluding and seducing spirits and doctrines that demons teach."
>
> —1 Timothy 4:1

These seducing spirits are at the root of the mass conditioning of the world's youth via diabolical productions like Twilight and Harry Potter. Such spirits have long been active and they are using many human agents as channels to convey their lies in their effort to transform Western civilization's collective worldview through mass media. Even the idea in the Wizard of Oz, that there are both "good" and "bad" witches, was channeled through an occultist by the name of Frank Baum (1851–1919).

Baum, who authored the Wizard of Oz, and converted it into a stage play before it became one of the most popular movies of all time, claimed, "There is a strong tendency in modern novelists toward introducing some vein of mysticism or occultism into their writings." The Annotated Wizard of Oz, Baum, an occultist who belonged to Helena Blavatsky's Theosophical Society (Blavatsky, like Aleister Crowley, claimed that Satan was good), used his writings to promote Theosophical views of magic and the occult. Baum claimed that he had channeled the Wizard of Oz, "It was pure inspiration.... It came to me right out of the blue. I think that sometimes the Great Author has a message to get across and He has to use the instrument at hand. I happened to be that medium, and I believe the magic key was given me to open the doors to sympathy and understanding, joy, peace and happiness." (Michael Patrick Hearn edition; The Annotated Wizard of Oz, New York: Clarkson N. Potter, 1973)

Baum's channeled message doesn't only teach children that there are "good" witches, but the message of Glenda (the "good" witch) to Dorothy was that she didn't have to look outside herself for answers.

"You've always had the power…" Glenda reveals to Dorothy. This, my friend, is basically the same message that is conveyed throughout the occult-based movies of our day, en masse, i.e., "We don't need to turn to God; we already have the power within. We need only tap into this latent power through meditation, incantations, contemplative prayer, etc." Lest we think that such messages carry little influence, I counter with Oprah Winfrey as "Exhibit A"! When explaining the origins of her greatest spiritual teaching she said, "Although I meditate every day and I pray every night and I read spiritual material, my greatest teaching is The Wizard of Oz… [The good witch says to Dorothy] 'You've always had the power my dear. You've always had the power.' That good witch, she's my girl!" Tragically, Oprah has become the most effective televangelist on TV, as she turns millions of unsuspecting souls toward an occult worldview through her promotion of books like The Secret by Rhonda Byrne and A New Earth by Eckhart Tolle. As you can see, young people are not the only ones being indoctrinated with last day's doctrines of demons!

Twilight and a Terrifying Spirit

Very few people are aware of the shocking truth that both Stephanie Meyer, who authored the Twilight saga, and J. K. Rowling, who authored the Harry Potter series, appear to have channeled their novels as evil spirits directed them. Like Rowling, Meyer has set her sights on our vulnerable youth; the Wall Street Journal reported, "Twilight has targeted the collective soul of teenage America, and will surely have its way." Meyer claims that she was compelled to write Twilight after the story was first communicated to her through a dream in June of 2003. Meyer admitted: "I woke up (on that June 2nd) from a very vivid dream. In my dream, two people were having an intense conversation in a meadow in the woods. One of these people was just your average girl. The other person was fantastically beautiful, sparkly, and a vampire. They were discussing the difficulties inherent in the facts that A) they were falling in love with each other while B) the vampire was particularly attracted to the scent of her blood, and was having a difficult time restraining himself from killing her immediately… I typed out as much as I could remember, calling the characters 'he' and 'she.'" (Source: www.stepheniemeyer.com)

This dream was so significant to the Twilight saga, that Meyer produced a transcript of her dream in Chapter 13 of her book, Twilight, entitled "Confessions." Meyer claims that sometime after she "received" the revelatory dream she heard incessant voices in her head that wouldn't stop until she would type, "Bella and Edward [the vampire] were, quite literally, voices in my head. They simply wouldn't shut up. I'd stay up as late as I could stand trying to get all the stuff in my mind typed out, and then crawl, exhausted, into bed … only to have another conversation start in my head." So furiously did Meyer's dark occult story pour forth that she said at times, "I couldn't type fast enough." She finished the dark tale, though it was her first book, in just three months. Meyer has also said, "I'm greatly looking forward to finally having Twilight on the shelves, and more than a little frightened, too. Overall, it's been a true labor of love, love for Edward and Bella and all the rest of my imaginary friends, and I'm thrilled that other people get to meet them now." Meyer also stated that the characters in Twilight "were so real to me, that I wanted other people to know them." Sadly, if the truth was known, and Twilight fans were truly aware of the dark and malignant nature of the 'real' forces behind the Twilight saga, they would run—and not walk—to the nearest exit! It appears as though the spirit entity appearing as Edward to Meyer in her dreams, and communicating to her when she was conscious, revealed more about his true nature than Meyer had bargained for.

Meyer confessed to Entertainment Weekly:

"I actually did have a dream after Twilight was finished of Edward coming to visit me—only I had gotten it wrong and he did drink blood like every other vampire and you couldn't live on animals the way I'd written it. We had this conversation and he was terrifying." A demon by any other name is still a demon! Rather than being the "good" vampire demon that is able to restrain from drinking Bella's blood, like the demons of the past that demanded the blood of children through child sacrifice, it is apparent that the spirit entities behind Twilight are the same old devils after all!

Meyer and Mormon Gnosticism

It may be significant that Stephanie Meyer chose a woman holding an apple for the front cover of Twilight, an ancient symbol of the forbidden fruit partaken by Eve, as she rebelled against her Creator and sought the position of God Himself. While we cannot be sure just what kind of fruit was on the tree of knowledge, the apple has become a popular depiction of the forbidden fruit that Satan used to deceive Eve. Meyer, who is a Mormon, may see the apple the way many leading Mormons and Satanists of the past did. Like ancient Gnosticism and the new spirituality, Mormonism teaches that one may become a god through secret knowledge. Ancient Gnostics venerated the serpent and celebrated Eve's partaking of the forbidden fruit in Eden. In the Mormon Church, achieving godhood comes through the temple endowment and secret Mormon rituals.

Tragically, Mormon leaders, like their Gnostic predecessors, have twisted the Genesis account and made Eve's fall, when partaking of the forbidden fruit, a heroic step... upward to godhood. Mormon leaders have contradicted God's own testimony as recorded in the book of Genesis and have taught that Satan told Eve the truth in offering humanity deification. Brigham Young, the most revered prophet in Mormonism after Joseph Smith, echoed the lie of Satan in Eden when he declared: "The devil told [Eve] the truth [about godhood]... I do not blame Mother Eve. I would not have had her miss eating the forbidden fruit for anything in the world." (Deseret News, June 18, 1873, from the pulpit of the Mormon Tabernacle in Salt Lake City on June 8, 1873).

Former LDS President, Joseph Fielding Smith, declared:

"The fall of man came as a blessing in disguise... I never speak of the part Eve took in this fall as a sin, nor do I accuse Adam of a sin... it is not always a sin to transgress a law...We can hardly look upon anything resulting in such benefits as a sin." (Joseph Fielding Smith, Doctrines of Salvation, Vol. 1, pp. 113–115)

Sterling Sill, Assistant to the Council of the Twelve Mormon Apostles proclaimed:

"This old sectarian doctrine, built around the idea of man's natural depravity and weakness inherited from Adam, is at the root of innumerable problems among us. Adam was one of the greatest men who has ever lived upon the earth… Adam fell, but he fell in the right direction. He fell toward the goal… Adam fell, but he fell upward." (Deseret News, Church Section, July 31, 1965, p. 7)

Like ancient Gnosticism, Mormonism has taught that Adam's disobedience to God and obedience to Satan opened not only his eyes, but his potential to realize "God consciousness" and true joy. Such teaching, which makes the serpent a savior, is reflected in the Mormon Scriptures written in the 19th century, "And in that day Adam blessed God… saying… for because of my transgression my eyes are opened and in this life I shall have joy." (Pearl of Great Price, Book of Moses 5:10–11), and "Adam fell that men might be; and men are, that they might have joy." (The Book of Mormon, 2 Nephi 2:22–25)

The apostle Paul warned the early Christians that they were to beware lest Satan seek to seduce them in the same way he seduced Eve: "But I am afraid that as the serpent deceived Eve by his cunning, your thoughts will be led astray from a sincere and pure devotion to Christ."—2 Corinthians 11:3.

Harry's Head Games

The first book of the Series, entitled "Harry Potter and the Sorcerer's Stone", find the orphan, Harry Potter, embarking into a new realm when he is taken to "Hogwarts School of Witchcraft and Wizardry." At this occult school, Harry Potter learns how to obtain and use witchcraft equipment. Harry also learns a new vocabulary, including words such as "Azkaban", "Circe", "Draco", "Erised", "Hermes", and "Slytherin"; all of which are names of real devils or demons. These are not characters of fiction! When it comes to real witches, they learn about two sides of "the force". When witches have real sabats, esbats, and meet as a coven, they greet each other by saying "blessed be", and when they part they say "the force be with you". Both sides of this force are Satan. High level witches believe that there are seven satanic princes and the seventh, which is assigned to Christians, has no name. In coven meetings, he is called "the nameless one." In the Harry Potter books, there is a character called "Voldemort." The pronunciation guide says of this being "He who must not be named." On July 8th 2010 at midnight, bookstores everywhere were stormed by millions of children to obtain the fourth book of the series known as "Harry Potter and the Goblet of Fire." I remember my Dad buying a voucher ahead of time so that I could get the newest installment of my favorite book series. I was 10 years old at the time and had no idea what these books would lead me to over the course of my life. These books were taken into homes everywhere with a real evil spirit following each copy to curse the children and their families. Looking back, I never had a chance to get away from this garbage. I loved these books and movies growing up. I remember having a program in school called "accelerated reading". In the program, students were required to read books from the school library. When we read a book, we would take a test of comprehension on the class computer. Each book varied in how many points we could score and it usually depended on how big the book was. The bigger the book, the more points you received. To compound on that, the more points you received, the better the prizes you would get at the end of the quarter. You can guess what happened next. I read all of the harry potter books because they were worth the most points! I wasn't the only one, every kid I knew read these books and we were rewarded for our obedience. The shame! Harry Potter books have taken the world of children's fantasy literature by storm. They call it fantasy literature for the sake of the public school system but let's just call it what it is "witchcraft". Over 500 million of these books have been sold in over 40 languages. One study shows that over half of the children in the western world have read at least one of the potter books, many reported rereading each book several times (I was one of them). Witchcraft now has the complete package. Starting in kindergarten with Harry Potter and TV witch shows, children are led on to the horror movies and hundreds of Wicca and Pagan websites. When they thirst for more power, high school and college Wicca covens are available. In the adult world, corporations are hiring New Age practitioners to provide seminars in sensitivity training, stress relief, and self-improvement for employees. The bottom line is a hunger for power. Harry Potter and the rest of witchcraft promises that power. But in the end, they discover that Satan is really in charge of the power and uses it like cheese in a mouse trap. This makes me think of saying "the early bird gets the worm, but the second mouse gets the cheese". Maybe it's not a bad idea to stand back and just observe what is going on before partaking in these witchcraft rituals. Just look at famous magicians who summon demons to perform for their audiences. Some go on to have successful careers like Chris Angel, David Blaine, ETC. These madmen will do insane things that boggle the minds of unbelievers of Jesus. Everything goes well and then one day they get an idea to do something really idiotic. It's only a matter of time before David and Chris suffer the same fate as so many magicians before them. Through Harry's world of sorcery, children are learning what tools today's witches and pagans use—supernatural imagination, spiritual concentration, wands, brooms, spells, and curses. Tragically, J. K. Rowling has revealed that her inspiration for Harry Potter also came in what appears to be spirit communication. This spirit communication happens to parallel that of Meyer's experience in chilling ways. Rowling's Harry Potter series is "the most popular children's series ever written," and as MTV acknowledged, has helped to initiate countless children into Wicca. Harry, as most know by now, was the victim of overbearing caregivers (called Muggles) until he found his calling as a sorcerer at Hogwarts School of Witchcraft and Wizardry. While the Twilight saga has seduced young people into an occult worldview, through romance, Harry Potter seduces young people into Wicca and other neo-pagan worldviews and practices through the lure of occult power and the lie that you, too, can become like God.

Rowling admitted that the initial story of Harry Potter, as well as many of the novel's characters, was communicated to her through a stream of consciousness… "Harry as a character came fully formed, as did the idea for his sidekicks, the characters of Ron and Hermione, who is the brains of the threesome," she said. "It started with Harry, then all these characters and situations came flooding into my head." (Boston Globe, January 3, 1999, Massachusetts USA)

Rowling describes the way she writes at times as though she is only taking notes of things she sees and hears in visions, "I see a situation and then I try to describe it as vividly as I can." (January Profile: J. K. Rowling, by Linda Richards, Source: www.januarymagazine.com)

In Hogwarts School of Witchcraft and Wizardry, Rowling has a special class where one may learn to communicate with spirits by tapping into their "mind's eye." This is interesting because this is the way Rowling describes receiving revelation in regard to her Potter series, "I have a very visual imagination. I see it, then, I try to describe what is in my mind's eye." (The Associated Press, Sheila Norman-Culp, New York, Source: www.turkishdailynews.com)

For Rowling, it all started on a train. It was 1990, and she was traveling from Manchester to London, "The character of Harry just strolled into my head… I really did feel he was someone who walked up and introduced himself in my mind's eye," said Rowling, "I was staring out the window" she says, "and the idea for Harry just came. He appeared in my mind's eye, very fully formed." (Reuters, "Harry Potter 'Strolled into My Head'" July 17, 2000)

For Rowling, spirit communication with the dark forces is beyond visual, as she admits when she writes dialogue between characters, she is simply taking notes from what she hears audibly:

"And I do love writing dialog. Dialog comes to me as though I'm just overhearing a conversation." (January Profile: J. K. Rowling, by Linda Richards, Source: w ww.januarymagazine.com

Growing up reading the harry potter books and watching the movies with my father, I adopted the belief that there was good magic (white) and dark magic (black). I was deceived into thinking that there was good and evil magic. This however, is not factual and God clearly states that all witchcraft is an abomination in his sight. What I didn't realize until later in my spiritual journey, is that God hates witchcraft is because it hurts us. It's why he warns us multiple times in his word that we should not practice any type of sorcery. According to God, there is life and death in the power of the tongues.

In new age lingo it means that we can "create our world" with our words.

Those who desire to remain true to Christ must be ever vigilant to discern the tactics of the devil, lest they succumb to devilish doctrines taught by seducing spirits. While Satan appears to reward few of his servants well (albeit, temporarily)… Stephanie Meyer went from never having written a single book to becoming a renowned author. J. K. Rowling went from rags to riches, from collecting welfare stamps to becoming the "richest woman in the world"… Jesus warned, "What profit will a person have if he gains the whole world and forfeits his soul?" (Mark 8:36) Jesus also warned of the impending judgment, "but whoever causes one of these little ones who believe in me to stumble, it would be better for him to have a heavy millstone hung around his neck, and to be drowned in the depth of the sea." (Matthew 18:6)

The One True Light

Dear reader, people are unaware that there is a spiritual battle between good and evil because so many are blinded to the fact that they themselves, either knowingly or unknowingly, have become participants. The sad and tragic result is that many have been deceived to the point of becoming spiritually blind.

I too was as blind as a bat when it came to spiritual things and consequently, opened myself up to satanic forces while "innocently" seeking to tap into the power of the "subconscious" mind. In doing so, I rejected the Creator and His Word, the Bible, and my rebellious quest opened me up to a Pandora's box of dark satanic forces that I had no idea existed. Thankfully, when I came to realize that both God and Satan existed, and that the living God inspired the Bible, I turned from my sinful rebellion against my Maker and cried out to the Lord Jesus Christ. Praise God, He was more than faithful to fulfill His promise that, "Whoever calls upon the name of the Lord shall be saved." (Romans 10:13) Hallelujah! God mercifully vanquished the dark forces that sought to control my life and gave me a place in His eternal kingdom. He commissioned me to "Have nothing to do with the fruitless deeds of darkness, but rather expose them." (Ephesians 5:11), and commissioned me to preach the Good News of salvation through the Lord Jesus Christ.

Dear friend, I encourage you to turn from Twilight to the true light, Jesus Christ, who died for the sins of the world and rose from the dead to conquer death and the grave. Jesus said, "I am the Light of the world; he who follows me will not walk in the darkness, but will have the Light of life." (John 8:12) No matter the depths of your sin against God, He loves you and is standing by with open arms to welcome you into His eternal family. (Luke 15:11–32)

Jesus Christ said:

> "For God so loved the world that He gave His only Son, that whoever believes in Him should not perish, but have eternal life. For God did not send His Son into the world to condemn the world, but in order that the world might be saved through Him. Whoever believes in Him is not condemned; but whoever does not believe is condemned already, because he has not believed in the name of the only Son of God. And this is the judgment, that the light has come into the world, and people loved the darkness rather than the light; because their works were evil. For everyone who does wicked things hates the light, and does not come to the light, lest his works should be exposed. But whoever does what is true comes to the light, so that it may be clearly seen that his works have been carried out in God."
>
> —John 3:16–21

The Lord Jesus Christ warned in the book of Revelation that at the Great White Throne Judgment, just before He creates a new heaven and a new earth, all those who practice magic arts (i.e., Wiccans, New Agers, astrologers, neo-pagans, etc.) are going to be sentenced to the lake of fire:

"The cowardly, the unbelieving, the vile, the murderers, the sexually immoral, those who practice magic arts, the idolaters and all liars— their place will be in the fiery lake of burning sulfur. This is the second death."

—Revelation 21:8

Please know that if you are reading this book, it is not by accident... God, in His great love and providence, is giving you an opportunity to see through Satan's lies and come to the knowledge of the truth, just as He did for me! If you want to escape eternal judgment and a Christless eternity in Hell forever, you must turn from your sinful life and put your trust in the Lord Jesus Christ, who gave Himself for your sins on the cross.

While the demonic vampire-like gods of the pagans demand the blood of their victims and little children, the Creator God did just the opposite and became a man and shed His blood sacrificially on the cross in your place. Dear friend, Jesus Christ, not Edward, Harry Potter, or any other demonic caricature should be permitted to divert your attention from the true lover of your soul. He made you and loves you. His story, which is true history, is beyond anything any Hollywood script writer could ever write. He is waiting patiently for you to cry out to Him for eternal life, before it is too late. All you have to do is seek Him now in repentant faith through prayer and He will fulfill His promise, "I will never turn away anyone who comes to me." (John 6:37b)

God's Word reveals, "The Son of God appeared for this purpose, to destroy the works of the devil." (1 John 3:8) If you are turning from darkness to light, it is imperative that you make sure that you renounce the satanic strongholds that have held you in bondage. This was the practice of the early Christians as recorded in the book of Acts:

"And a number of those who had practiced magic arts brought their books together and burned them in the sight of all. And they

76

counted the value of them and found it came to
fifty thousand pieces of silver."

—Acts 19:19

If you are turning to Christ now, I want to encourage you to renounce the works of darkness and begin reading God's Word, continue to pray, and find a church that sincerely submits to God's Word in faith and practice. If you are already a Christian, I would like to encourage you to get this book into the hands of as many people as possible so we may rescue the many millions of people who are being led into the occult through the popular movies and productions mentioned earlier.

May God give you the grace and wisdom to walk worthy of the Heavenly calling we share in our beloved Savior, the Lord Jesus Christ!

The Hollywood Illusion

Morpheus: "This is your last chance. After this, there is no turning back. You take the blue pill—the story ends, you wake up in your bed and believe whatever you want to believe. You take the red pill—you stay in Wonderland and I show you how deep the rabbit-hole goes."

"Whoever has ears, let them hear".

—(Matthew 11:15)

Speaking of the Matrix, I'd like to talk about Keanu Reeves who plays Neo. What an amazing job he did with the martial arts in that film. I can only imagine the discipline and hours of practice that it took to perform like that. I'm sure it was a pretty big sacrifice for the 53-year-old Canadian actor. What's interesting about the film is its parallel to Jesus. Neo plays "the one" or "the Messiah "and ends up sacrificing his life to save humanity. He's actually portraying Jesus in the movie.

Morpheus represents John the Baptist who is a voice in the wilderness preparing the way for Neo. Zion represents God's holy city and his people. The Merovingian represents the devil and agent smith represents sin. At the end of the movie, neo becomes sin (agent smith attempts to kill him and copy himself into him) but he couldn't hold him or destroy him. Hmm coincidence? The synopsis of the movie is this "the world is born into bondage". The majority of the people are completely imperceptive to the world they are living in, which is a counterfeit reality. Much like our own world, the deceptions become more and more strange. With that being said, I want to point out another sacrifice the actor has made recently.

This stand that he made was not for money, fame, or hopes of creating another blockbuster film. In an interview he exposed the Hollywood pedophiles who kill babies, eat their flesh and drink their blood.—Nov 20, 2017.

Claims their devotion to Lucifer has been an open secret known by many, but it is what goes on behind closed doors that will make one shutter. According to Reeves, Hollywood elites us "the blood of babies to get high". He warned that "these people believe the more innocent the child, and the more it suffered before it died, the better the high". Speaking from Milan, Italy, where Reeves now designs motorbikes, he continued, "The revelations that are coming out of Hollywood now, I'm telling you, they are just the tip of the iceberg. Children are revered, they are put on pedestals, but they are also tortured, raped, murdered, and consumed in various way. They are a currency. And I'm sad to say this practice seems to be becoming more and more open in those circles in recent years". Reeves has left the grips of Hollywood and co-founded a motorcycle in Milan, explaining that he is "building a future" where he is free from Hollywood's shackles". He spoke with absolute revulsion about "the place of the child in Hollywood". He is one of the few who put his morals above fame and fortune. Most of these people will do ANYTHING to reach the top, even if it means joining a satanic cult that eats the flesh of babies and drinks their blood. He added that it was "inconceivable" that anybody could "be so selfish as to destroy a young person's life for their own personal pleasure." He called them "sociopaths", and his claims mirror those of Justin Bieber. "They see it as the ultimate high", Reeves said. "They say it gives them life. The more the child suffered, the more fear and hormonal adrenaline it had in its system at the time of death, the stronger the effect on the people who consume that blood. They live for this stuff" Hollywood is full of these predators. According to Reeves, they carry bottles of blood around and call it "red wine". From what I understand there is a supply chain that delivers young children on the regular. I've heard them refer to times of famine, times of feast". Reeves further goes on to say "for a long time, I thought it was a joke, or coded language. I didn't think it could be what it seemed to be". Keanu explained "but then I got invited to a well-known mogul's mansion and he had two dead babies in his fridge. A white on and a brown one. I freaked out, I broke this guy's things, and I broke his nose. I called the police and they said I sounded crazy. More than likely the officer was paid to keep quiet. That is how things work there". Even though Reeves was a top producer in Hollywood, he kept to himself, and kept the secret locked up inside. He continued, "I Just hope with all the dirt coming out of Hollywood now, people will start to wake up and realize the extent of what is going on there. People can't be expected to take it all in at once. Until then, these people will keep getting away with it. Sometimes I dream about Hollywood burning to the ground." It really shocks me to hear what Reeves says about Hollywood and the elite. I don't know about you guys, but when I see movies like "twilight" and Netflix shows like the ""the Santa Clarita diet", I wonder. I can't help but wondering about the merit of these claims made by Keanu, Justin, and other celebrities. But I ask myself this question, "Why would they lie about something so evil and deranged"? I know they are actors and performers, but could they really concoct a story about people drinking the blood of infants? Who has that type of imagination to make up such a tale? Not me! I have a pretty big imagination folks, but I don't come up with stories of blood necklaces or treating babies like a form of currency. It's too much. That is where discernment comes in to guide us. Discernment comes from the Holy Spirit. Pray this prayer aloud:

Father God, I ask you to grant me the gift of your Holy Spirit. To cleanse me of all demons and to lead me into all matters of my heart. Father God reveal to me all demonic forces that I carry and

Chapter 11

A little tip from heaven

"Draw near to God and He will draw near
to you."

—James 4:8

"Pain is proof to you that you have something worth praising"
(God)

"What do you mean by that?" Can you give me an example?
(Me)

"Absolutely, let's use the death of a loved one. Say you lose someone that was close to you. Then pain sets in your heart, right? (God)

"Right. And then? (Me)

"Then that is your proof that you can still praise me" (God)

"I don't understand" (Me)

"My son, what is the opposite of pain?" (God)

"Joy and Love I suppose" (Me)

"Yes, so why would a person be in pain after losing a loved one"
(God)

"Oh wow!! Because that love was taken away!?? (Me)

"Yes, so you see, there is always something worth praising.
Remember that every person is operating in one of two kingdoms.
Either the devil's kingdom or my kingdom. In the enemy's kingdom
there is destruction, lust, depression, addiction, rape, suicide, murder, hate, lying, stealing, jealousy, strife, and division. In my king-

dom there is peace, joy, love, forgiveness, abundance, patience, and longsuffering. It is perfectly natural to mourn a loss. Pain is proof to indicate to you that you lost something special. But will you praise me when you have experienced that loss? Will you remember all of the good memories and blessings that you did have with that person? Will you choose to be angry for the time that you didn't get to spend with that person, or will you be grateful for the time that you did have? I gave that person to you and blessed you with those fond memories. (God)

Chapter 12

Catching fire

"The most powerful weapon on earth is the human soul on fire"

I was asked to go minister to the homeless on the streets of Louisville Kentucky by a church member and friend of mine. After a few weeks of thinking I wasn't good enough to go out and preach the gospel, I agreed to go with Caleb to reach out to the homeless people of Louisville. Johnathan, another good friend of mine, went with us so there were three. Caleb had a gift of preaching and Johnathan had a gift of operating in the prophetic. I always called him "Black Moses" because of his dreadlocks and his relationship with God.

Ha-ha! So, in the summer months of 2018, all three of us rode out to downtown Louisville looking for who we could help and serve. On the car ride there, we all began praying for hedges of protection around us, guidance from the holy spirit, who to talk to, and rebuking all demonic spirits that would try to hinder us or the holy spirit in any way. I was in the backseat praying in tongues when we pulled up to our stop. "These two guys don't need me" I thought to myself. "Why am I here"? Then the spirit of the Lord spoke to me and said "to bring the fire" We met many people that day. Some were open to Jesus and others weren't. We came across a small group of men and women living right next to an overpass living in tents. For being homeless, they kept their area pretty clean and seemed to be very content where they were. there was plenty of grass and trees in the small area where they were staying. We asked everyone if they needed prayer for anything and only one man said yes. No real miracles happened other than just being friendly, kind smiles, and offering prayer and encouragement. After the overpass, we made our way to a new area. It was more in the heart of the city under a bridge where we saw a real move of God. There were about 20 people or so living under this bridge and they surprisingly had electricity. Someone had run a very long extension cord to a generator nearby. One by one we asked people if they needed prayer and gave them our testimonies of being homeless ourselves and overcoming addiction. We let them know about Jesus and how he had saved us from our burdens. Most people were pleasant but not very interested. One man was the antithesis of interested. He was about 6 foot 7 inches tall if I had to guess. He denied wanting prayer when we first talked to him. After his refusal we said "be blessed" and moved on to someone else and began talking with them. while in the middle of the conversation he came up and said something random to distract us from our conversation with another gentleman. I asked him "hey would you like prayer for anything?" this time he said "yes for prosperity".

Excited, Johnathan and I put our hands on his shoulders (we had to reach up because of his height) and I began to pray in English:

"Heavenly father, I thank you for (forgetting his name) and bringing us together, Lord I pray that you would reveal yourself to him in a very real way in Jesus name, and Jesus I also ask you to bless…" and before I could get out the words of prosperity and blessing for this man's prayer, he immediately hit me in the shoulder and said with anger "I didn't ask you for Jesus!!!!!!!! I asked you for prosperity and money!!

Without missing a beat, my friend Johnathan replied to him saying "Yeah, but Jesus provides prosperity!"

I laughed when he said that and the man walked off immediately as if we had just wronged him in some way. Caleb commented and said what we all knew to be true…

"Antichrist spirit" isn't it interesting? How can a name offend people so much? In all fairness people get upset over the silliest things but nothing causes more controversy than the name "Jesus". It's why the man stormed off, because of the spirit that was on him.

After that we had decided it was enough for one day, but God wasn't done. On our way down we saw a middle-aged black man whose name was "Teddy".

Teddy was clearly intoxicated but coherent enough to speak. We asked if he needed prayer for anything and his response to me was staggering "yeah, pray for my mom, she has cancer". My heart was moved and I believe my fellow constituents felt the same. Before Johnathan, Caleb, and I began to pray for Teddy, we had him come down from under the bridge onto flat ground. He was too wobbly and tipsy for us to pray for him on the concrete slanted surface. We began praying in English for his mother to be healed from cancer and then something shifted. I felt extremely warm and like fire had hit me in my body. "Pray for fire for teddy". I heard in my spirit.

Immediately after that word jumped into my spirit, I began praying in tongues and the interpretation of the prayer was "father bring your fire upon this man teddy. Fire! Fire! Fire!" Caleb then began praying in tongues too. After about 30–45 seconds, the spirit of the Lord dropped a word unto Johnathan saying "his disc in his back is injured". all the while this is happening, Teddy is swaying side to side like in a trance. When Johnathan told him what the Lord said about his back, he was shocked and said "I haven't talked to anyone about that!!!!" What happened next surprised all three of us. Teddy started opening up his eyes like he was sobering up. it's worth noting here that when we first saw teddy, we knew he was drunk and his eyes were really heavy and almost closed. he had a tall liquor can in his hand when we first approached him. After the revelation about Teddy's back was revealed, his eyes began opening. We could clearly see him sobering up right before our eyes. God wasn't done yet! All three of us were still praying and then another thing happened. After Teddy's eyes became clear, the fire of God hit him and he started smiling and laughing.

He stood straight up and said his back wasn't hurt anymore! But God wasn't done yet! Then Teddy became what believers of Jesus would call being drunk in the Holy Spirit! God is good! So,

God healed teddy's back, sobered him up from alcohol, and got him drunk in the holy spirit! Needless to say, when we said our goodbyes to Teddy, he walked away skipping with joy and healing! Now I know why I'm alive. Three of us made a difference that day...

"Though one may be overpowered, two can defend themselves. A cord of three strands is not quickly broken."

—Ecclesiastes 4:12

Chapter 13

The Challenge

Here is a 12-day plan that you can take to get started towards freedom from any situation that you are struggling with. I used a colon cleansing product while fasting called "super colon cleanse". It was a little over $10 and well worth the investment. Our bodies are extremely overworked with toxins, and we wonder why we have trouble or lack energy throughout the day.

This is by no means a quick spiritual fix. This is merely to get you started in having your own relationship with God.

I've been high. I've been drunk. I've been both high and drunk but nothing compares to euphoria of God's presence when he shows up wherever you are. This is not some voodoo or witchcraft ritual.

Fasting and prayer will change your life and you'll meet God for yourself if you want to. It opens the door for you if you really want to know the truth about God and your life.

When you take one step towards God, he takes two towards you. When I started, I MADE IT A POINT to seek God early in the morning (some days it was as early as 5am). In the bible it tells us to seek God early in the morning. When I was on this fast/cleanse, on the 7th day, I had the vision of the jezebel spirit that had attached itself to me through sexual promiscuity. Yes, men can be Jezebels too. It is crucial you don't give up and that you keep getting up to pray every day. I don't understand why it works, but seeking God early in morning seems to provide supernatural breakthroughs and your day goes way smoother. I was praying at least 1 to 2 hours every day. (some days it was as early as 5am). In the bible it tells us to seek God early in the morning. When I was on this fast/cleanse, on the 7th day, I had the vision of the jezebel spirit that had attached itself to me through sexual promiscuity. Yes, men can be Jezebels too. It is crucial you don't give up and that you keep getting up to pray every day. I don't understand why it works, but seeking God early in morning seems to provide supernatural breakthroughs and your day goes way smoother. I was praying at least 1 to 2 hours every day.

God will honor that I promise you. It doesn't matter what the sin is, it can be pornography, drugs, sex outside of marriage, alcohol, ying, operating in witchcraft, stealing, or anything that doesn't line up with God's word. You can lay it down right here. Speak these twelve steps out loud with your mouth (very important). On each day, write down your own personal thoughts and notes about your situation. Keep in mind that I'm not asking you to go to a church or say 10 our fathers and 20 hail marys. I'm just here encouraging you to seek God on your own. He met me where I was, and he loved me too much to leave me where I was. Ask him to help you in any area of your life that is important to you and find scriptures pertaining to your situation.

The last point I want to make, is to be honest with him. He already knows what you're going through anyway. Speak to him about what you are really concerned about. The idea is to dig deep into your heart and tell God what matters most to you. Seek him on your own, in a quiet and peaceful place, and you will find him! Keep this in mind, God took the desire of drugs and alcohol out of me in one single night. I haven't touched the stuff since and have zero desire to. I was at the baseball field alone when it happened and my life hasn't been the same since. When God's presence showed up on that field, I knew he was real and nobody could tell me any different. I didn't meet church, a preacher, or religion…I met him! You can too!!

He promises in his word that says "If we confess our sin to him, he is faithful and just to forgive us, and cleanse us from all unrighteousness".

I hope this book helped you in some way, God bless you!

Day 1: Admit: We admit we are powerless over our addictions, brokenness, and sinful patterns—that in our own power our lives are unmanageable.

Biblical foundation: "For I know that nothing good dwells in me, that is, in my flesh. For I have the desire to do what is right, but not the ability to carry it out" (Romans 7:18)

Prayer: Dear God, if recovery is available for me please help me, find freedom."

(Write down your addictions or struggles that weigh you down. You may not be comfortable telling somebody about it just yet, but just write it down in this book and make a confession to God that you acknowledge this part about yourself. He already knows about it anyway!)

Day 2: Believe: we come to believe that God is the one whose power can fully restore us.

Biblical foundation: "Bless the Lord, O my soul, and forget not all his benefits, who forgives all your iniquity, who heals all your diseases, who redeems your life from the pit, who crowns you with steadfast love and mercy, who satisfies you with good so that your youth is renewed like the eagle's" (Psalm 103:2–5)

_____

_____

_____

_____

_____

_____

Prayer: Dear God, help me understand your unconditional love. Thank you for loving me as I am with all my faults and sins. Open my heart to know and accept the love and grace that you have for me.

Day 3: Trust: We decide to trust God with our lives and wills by accepting his grace through Jesus Christ.

Biblical foundation: "But God, being rich in mercy because of the great love with which he loved us, even when we were dead in our trespasses, made us alive together with Christ-by grace you have been saved" (Ephesians 2:4–5)

_____

_____

_____

_____

_____

_____

_____

Prayer: Dear God, please keep me sober for the next 24 hours by your perfect strength. Teach me to seek you and your will today. Thank you for helping me.

(Today, call someone you trust like a family member or friend and tell them you are committing to be sober for the next 24 hours).

Day 4: Inventory: We make a searching and fearless moral inventory of ourselves.

Biblical foundation: "Behold, you delight in truth in the inward being, and you teach me wisdom in the secret heart (Psalm 51:6)

_____

_____

_____

_____

_____

_____

_____

Prayer: Dear God, I ask you to give me a safe place where I can heal from my struggles and pain in life. Please give me the strength and discipline to attend a Holy Spirit filled church consistently. Remove any obstacles that would hinder me from attending.

Day 5: Confess: We confess to God, to ourselves, and to another human being the exact nature of our sins.

Biblical foundation: "But if we walk in the light, as he is in the light, we have fellowship with one another, and the blood of Jesus his Son cleanses us from all sin. If we say we have no sin, we deceive ourselves, and the truth is not in us. If we confess our sins, he is faithful and just to forgive us our sins and to cleanse us from all unrighteousness." (1 John 1:7–9)

_____

_____

_____

_____

_____

_____

_____

Prayer: Dear God, please help me realize that I am not alone. Please give me the courage to rely on you and others who you have put in my life to help me heal.

(When God brings you to a place where others are struggling the same battles, reach out to someone of the same sex about your struggle and share with them what it is. Exchange phone numbers or email with this one person so that you can encourage and pray for one another).

Day 6: Repent: We become entirely ready to turn away from our patterns of sin and turn to God.

Biblical Foundation: "So flee youthful passions and pursue righteousness, faith, love, and peace. Along with those who call on the Lord from a pure heart." (2 Timothy 2:22)

_____

_____

_____

_____

_____

_____

_____

Prayer: Father God, I ask you to bring to my attention, all of the things that I need to repent and let go of. Help me to see and understand my sin and what negative effects it has on my life. Lead me into the beautiful life you have planned for me.

In Jesus name.

Day 7: Follow: We humbly ask God's spirit to change our hearts and minds in order to follow Chris fully.

Biblical foundation: "but the fruit of the spirit of is love, joy, peace, patience, kindness, goodness, faithfulness, gentleness self-control: against such things there is no law. And those who belong to Christ Jesus have crucified the flesh with its passions and desires. If we live by the Spirit, let us also keep in step with the spirit." (Galatians 5:22–25)

_____

_____

_____

_____

_____

_____

_____

Prayer: "Where can I go from your spirit? Where can I flee from your presence? If I go up to the heavens you are there; If I make my bed in the depths, you are there."

(Do something Christ-like today. Go out and give an act of random kindness to someone. It can be someone you know or a stranger. Give something of yourself away whether it is your time, a donation, or some act of generosity without expecting anything in return. Ask God for an idea if you are unsure on what to do)

Day 8: Forgive: We forgive those who have harmed us and become willing to make amends to those we have harmed.

Biblical foundation: "Be kind to one another, tenderhearted, forgiving one another, as God in Christ forgave you. Therefore be imitators of God, as beloved children." (Ephesians 4:32–5:1)

_____

_____

_____

_____

_____

_____

_____

Prayer: Father God help me to forgive those who have hurt me in the past. Help me to truly forgive them so that you can move in and heal me.

In Jesus name.

Day 9: Amends: We make direct amends whenever possible, submitting to God, his word, and biblical counsel.

Biblical Foundation: "Repay no one evil for evil, but give thought to do what is honorable in the sight of all. If possible, so far as it depends on you, live peaceably with all." (Romans 12:17–18)

_____

_____

_____

_____

_____

_____

Prayer: Father God, Guide me and help me make amends with anyone and everyone that I need to make it right with. Grant me the strength and courage to admit my faults so that I can be reconciled with people and with you.

In Jesus Name.

Day 10: Continue: We continue to examine our lives and when we sin promptly confess and turn to walk with Christ.

Biblical Foundation: "Search me, O God, and know my heart! Try me and know my thoughts! And see if there be any grievous way in me, and lead me in the way everlasting! "(Psalm 139:23–24)

_____

_____

_____

_____

_____

_____

_____

Prayer: Father God, I ask that you wash away all of my sins with the blood of Jesus. Your word says that by his stripes I am healed. I thank you for your forgiveness and your grace.
In Jesus Name.

Day 11: Intimacy: We seek to deepen our relationship with God daily and depend on his power to do his will.

Biblical foundation: "And this is eternal life, that they know you the only true God, and Jesus Christ whom you have sent." (John 17:3)

_____

_____

_____

_____

_____

_____

_____

Prayer: Father God, help me to have true intimacy and relationship with you. Guide me and grant me revelation of your word so that I may know you and understand who you really are. Create a plan to help me progress in the things of you.

In Jesus name.

(Write down what you think true intimacy with God means. What does it look like? Feel like?

Sound like?) What do you imagine unconditional love to be like?)

Day 12: Regenerate: Because of our new lives in Christ, we carry God's message of reconciliation to others and practice these principles in every aspect of our lives.

Biblical foundation "Therefore, if anyone is in Christ, he is a new creation. The old has passed away; behold, the new has come. All this is from God, who through Christ reconciled us to himself and gave us the ministry of reconciliation." (2 Corinthians 5:17–18)

_____

_____

_____

_____

_____

_____

_____

Prayer: "Father God, thank you for your Holy Spirit and my new life in Christ. Help me to continue this daily practice of seeking you every morning and growing spiritually each and every day."

(Make a commitment to attend a Holy Spirit filled church every time the doors are open. Where ever there are two or more people gathered in his name, God will dwell in the midst. There is power in numbers!)

All who call on the name of the LORD shall be saved.

About the Author

Bobby Sky was born in Tulsa, Oklahoma, on December 11, 1989, and grew up in Fort Smith, Arkansas. He grew up in smoky pool halls, learning to yield a pool cue, and started winning adult pool tournaments at 9 years old. He grew up hearing stories of his parents' days of revelry with the Tyson family (chicken). Even though his parents endured great pains in their childhood, which transferred into their adult lives, Bobby grew up sensitive to the spiritual realm. To add to that, church and prayer life were nonexistent for this millennial growing up. It wouldn't be until after Bobby's teenage years of partying, rebellion, and near-fatal car accident at age 18, later in his life he would seek out spiritual truth. He looked and researched in practices such as the new age philosophy, Wicca, meditation, and Buddhism. Being left unfulfilled in all his searching, it wasn't until what he recalls as "the field" that would become the birthing ground of his greatest discovery in his life. He says, "God will meet us wherever we are, he did for me." Today he enjoys being outdoors, working as a caretaker for the mentally disabled, going to his church On Fire Christian Center (Louisville, Kentucky), and ministering the gospel to the homeless on the streets. He still occasionally shoots pool but humbly admits, "My 9 year old self would whoop me unto tears today!" His message is for the millennial generation who he says were deceived into practicing new age and Wicca. The American millennials are in trouble! The schools and media tricked us as children into believing a lie. I grew up reading all of the Harry Potter books and movies which led to more harmful things down the road in my own life. Millennials really are asleep like the people in The Matrix movie.

They have no clue what goes on in Hollywood, how music effects the subconscious mind, and how there is life and death in the power of the tongues. My sincere prayer is that my book will inspire and illuminate the truth so that they can make a choice for themselves. I didn't know any better back then and that's why I wrote this book. To give those who are searching for truth a chance to see what is real. God's secret is a 10-day plan that anyone can do. My only question is, are millennials brave enough? I sincerely hope so."

CPSIA information can be obtained
at www.ICGtesting.com
Printed in the USA
BVHW051112180822
644921BV00002B/252